Power Selling
An A to Z of Salesmanship

To Terry
with my very best
wishes and thanks for
your support over the years
Brendan Powell
Dec. 2000

Illustrations and front cover design by Samantha Brayford

British Library Cataloguing in Publication Data
Brendan F. Power
Power Selling an A to Z of Salesmanship
I. Title

ISBN 1 85609 155 4

While the principles discussed and the details given in this book are the product of careful study, the author and publisher cannot in any way guarantee the suitability of recommendations made in this book for individual problems, and they shall not be under any legal liability of any kind in respect of or arising out of the form or contents of this book or any error therein, or the reliance of any person thereon.

Power Selling
An A to Z of Salesmanship

by

Brendan Power

LONDON
WITHERBY & CO. LTD
32-36 Aylesbury Street,
London EC1R 0ET

1st EDITION 1998

WITHERBY

PUBLISHERS

ISBN 1 85609 155 4

Witherby & Co. Ltd.
32-36 Aylesbury Street
London EC1R 0ET

Tel No: 0171 251 5341
Fax No: 0171 251 1296

Introduction

This book has been written in such a way that you can read it from cover to cover or just dip in and out of various topics as you see fit. Each topic is an important part of the sales process but, at the same time, can stand alone.

Throughout the book I have used the masculine gender for ease of reading. For instance, I have referred to a "Salesman" but I am well aware that women make up a very large and important part of this country's sales force.

Those people who buy our products and services are given many names: customers, buyers, prospects and, unfortunately, even punters. The name I have chosen to use is clients. This is the name I use in my own business as I believe it helps to raise their importance in my mind and, of course, they are the most important people in our business.

Whether you are an old hand or a newcomer to sales I am sure you will find plenty of interest in this book and I do hope you get both benefit and pleasure from it.

BRENDAN POWER

For

Carole, Simon and Craig

About the Author

Brendan Power is recognised as one of the UK's leading motivational and inspirational speakers. He has addressed audiences in all kinds of businesses in more than twenty countries around the world.

Brendan was born in Fethard-on-Sea in the south east of Ireland and moved with his family to London while he was still at school. He has been involved in selling since he was fourteen. At that young age he obtained samples of personalised stationery from advertisers in the Exchange & Mart, and used them to sell the product door to door around his London home.

Leaving school he bypassed sales for a while and joined a leading firm of City stockbrokers. Looking for something to get him out of the office he moved to retail sales and spent some time working in both large and small outlets. Self-employment soon beckoned and he became a dance promoter and artist manager before moving on to join the pirate radio stations of the 1960's.

From Radio 270 off Scarborough, Brendan moved to Radio Antilles on the Caribbean island of Montserrat where he was both programme director and news editor before forsaking the microphone for the position of sales manager.

Back in the UK he was instrumental in the launch of BRMB, Birmingham's commercial radio station, where he spent three years, initially as a producer and laterly in sales. A short spell selling encyclopaedias preceded his move to the financial services business where he has been the recipient of numerous awards and honours.

In addition to his financial services practice, Brendan spent almost two decades on various committees of the Life Insurance Association culminating in three years as a director.

Contents

SALESMAN OF THE YEAR

1

ATTITUDE

"Pathetic attitudes are not in keeping with greatness." - Friedrich Nietzsche

It is indeed good fortune that "A" is the first letter of the alphabet. If it were not we would have to start this book out of order because I firmly believe that the most important component of selling, or any other business for that matter, is attitude. Without the right attitude everything else we do is meaningless.

It has been stated that something in the region of eighty-five percent of everything we do is determined by our attitude, which is good news because we have a choice. We can choose for ourselves whether our life is influenced by a positive attitude or a negative attitude. Just think what that means; you have total control over what happens in eighty-five percent of your life. Surely with that kind of power you can cope with the other fifteen percent, even though sometimes things do not quite go according to plan.

Perhaps you are thinking *"I can't do that because I don't have a positive attitude all the time"*. Well, there is no need to worry on that account because you are in good company. You see, possessing a positive attitude is not normal. Most people are brought up from childhood to think in negative terms and *not to have ideas beyond their station.* In other words, they have been told to be satisfied with what they have got and not to strive for something better, or for what may at first appear to be the impossible. And yet, even the seemingly impossible can be achieved with the right attitude; with a positive attitude. Fortunately, such an attitude is something which, even if you do not have it now, can be acquired. There is nothing complicated about it but, like everything else worthwhile, it does require some effort on your part.

The effort centres around positive thinking. Not just positive thinking however. On its own, positive thinking does not work. You could lie in bed all day thinking positively but at the end of the day you would still be in bed and nothing would have changed. The solution is positive thinking, coupled with action. You have to get out of bed and do something, nothing will ever happen until you take some kind of action.

If you do not currently have a positive attitude to life there are a number of things you can do to help you think and act more positively. Start by staying away from negative influences. Especially stay away from those people whose sole aim in life, whether they know it or not, appears to be to find the negative aspect in everything they see or do, and to encourage everybody else to do the same. Instead, mix with positive people and look for the positive aspects in everything that happens in your life. It will not always be immediately obvious, but there is a positive side to everything that happens. Finding it may well require a little of that effort I mentioned earlier, but I promise you it is an effort well worth making.

Read books on the subject, listen to tapes, attend seminars and benefit from the attitude and experience of the speakers. Although you may encounter some difficulties to start with, when you persevere and make it a habit it will change your whole approach to business, and to everything else in your life.

There is nothing new about what I am saying here. The knowledge has been with us for centuries, but it is only in the last two hundred years or so that it has come to the forefront. At the beginning of the 1900's the American philosopher and pragmatist William James wrote *"The greatest discovery of my generation is that human beings can alter their lives by altering their attitude of mind".* Although he was a few decades out on his timing of the discovery, the message is very straight forward. When you want to change your life, or your business, the only way to do it is by being prepared to change your attitude.

Bear in mind however that nothing in life is perfect. I can offer you no guarantee that a positive attitude will always work for you; but I can guarantee beyond any question that a negative attitude will work every time to your detriment.

2

ACTIVITY

"Every noble activity makes room for itself".- Ralph Waldo Emerson

Anybody who has ever worked at the sharp end of selling, knows that there are times for every sales person when business slows down. For some of them it will come to a virtual standstill. It does not matter how experienced the individual is, they still share the troughs with the peaks. The important difference is that with experience the troughs get shallower while the peaks get higher.

Your aim should be to ensure that when you next encounter those troughs, they are as shallow as possible. You do this by recognising what is happening and rectifying it before it is too late. Later on in this book we will see how record keeping can help in this area. Although there is no single reason for these troughs, there is a common denominator in the majority of cases. Lack of activity. Or more accurately, lack of productive activity.

It is all too easy to bury our heads in unproductive administration and paper work or to hide in front of a computer screen. You can keep yourself occupied for hours like that. These are tasks, however, which could and should be carried out by somebody else. Such jobs are a part of the sales process, but they are not your part. You do not expect your administrators, secretaries, receptionists or other back up staff to do your job, so why should you spend your time doing theirs. What I am saying here is nothing new, everybody knows it. Unfortunately knowing it is not the same as doing it, and it is still a trap into which we all fall time and again.

The questions we have to ask ourselves are: how do we avoid the trap and how do we turn activity into our constant ally to ensure there are less troughs? Some years ago I addressed the problem in a rather unusual manner; by spending what I considered at the time to be a significant sum of money. There is a maxim which, when you follow it, will keep you out of the trough. My solution was to commission a calligraphist to write that maxim out for me using gold leaf on hand made parchment paper. He did a tremendous job, and to finish it off I spent a similar sum of money having a frame made which matched the superb quality of his work.

That work of art now hangs on my office wall as a constant reminder to keep my activity productive. But why did I spend so much on it? The reason is simple. I wanted it to be important enough not to be ignored, because I believe the seven words it contains are vital for our success in sales. It says: *"Only do what only you can do."*

To stick to that maxim you have to ask yourself the question every day, and sometimes every hour: *"Am I doing what only I can do, or could what I am doing be done by somebody else?"* The answer will tell you whether your current activity is productive, or merely time consuming. If the answer is that it is just time consuming, or time wasting, then you have to make some changes. Start by delegating that particular task to somebody else and freeing more of your time to concentrate on what you do best; selling. There is an old saying that if, as a salesman, you are not telephoning for an appointment or presenting to a prospective client, you are not being productive. As a general rule of thumb it is well worth remembering.

The Pareto principle, or the 80/20 rule, says that 80% of your productivity comes from 20% of your activity. That being the case I recommend that you identify the 20% and then do more of it! And when it comes to planning your activity, remember what we said about attitude. A positive attitude will ensure high activity levels, high activity levels will improve your self-esteem which, in turn, will ensure a positive attitude, which will enable you to maintain your activity, and productivity, levels. The end result? Fewer troughs and more peaks.

3

BELIEF

"A belief is not merely an idea the mind possesses; it is an idea that possesses the mind." - *Robert Bolton*

Belief in yourself and your own ability is fundamental to your success. And it is essential that you demonstrate that self-belief in both your personal life and your business life. If you do not believe in your ability to succeed in any one area of your life, it will impact on all the other areas. After all, when you go to work, you do not step across a line and leave the rest of your world behind you. Your concerns and your problems will stay with you twenty four hours a day until you do something about them.

Initially you may have some doubts about your ability. There is nothing unusual about this. As we said before, it is a throw back to the negative input most of us received as children. The fact is, however, that everybody is far better and far more capable than they think they are. Everybody has the ability to achieve much more in life than they are currently achieving and the best way to do this is to put your positive beliefs to work, and eliminate your negative beliefs.

Your brain is the most sophisticated computer in the world but it has one major design fault. It is unable to distinguish between fact and fiction with the result that it believes everything you tell it. The pessimist, of course, will see that as a negative. The optimist, on the other hand, will take the positive approach, see it as a huge opportunity, and use it to his advantage. Whether you are computer literate or not, this is one computer that you really can learn to programme.

No special training is needed, you can do it by simple repetition. First of all, decide what it is you want to programme in. Then repeat it over and over and over until you convince your brain that you already have it. After that your brain will take over and work overtime to ensure you achieve it. The simplest, and most effective, way of doing this is by putting your targets, your goals, or your desires in writing and reading them, word for word, to yourself at least twice a day.

You can write your statements anywhere but I find that small white cards are best, the sort that are used for place names at the table. You can carry these cards with you in your pocket, your bag or your briefcase so they are close to hand at all times. Take them out and read them, word for word, whenever you have a few minutes to spare. When you are satisfied that you have achieved whatever it is that you have written on any particular card, file it away and replace it with another. Your brain can quite easily cope with fifteen or twenty different messages at a time.

There is however one very important point to bear in mind when you are preparing your cards. Whatever you write down must be a positive statement in the present tense. That means it must be written as though you have already achieved it. For instance, when you write *"I don't waste time on unnecessary paper work"*, your brain will treat it as a negative. It will ignore the *"don't"*, and go in the opposite direction, helping you instead to *"... waste time on unnecessary paper work"*. To achieve the result you want, a better statement to write would be *"I spend all my time on productive activities"*. This is a positive statement which concentrates on what you do want to happen, rather than what you do not want to happen. Wherever possible we should be even more specific: *"I see four prospects every day"*, *"I make ten telephone calls every day"*, *"I delegate all my unproductive work"* and so on. Remember, you are saying what you **want** to do in the future, not what you do now, but you are saying it as though you have already achieved it.

Does this work? That is a question I am frequently asked when I present this idea at my seminars. My answer is always the same, *"... do it for thirty days and then judge for yourself"*. I believe that by making this a habit you can change your life. However, like all success ingredients it will only work when you do it, and when you believe it will work. There is nothing difficult or complicated about it, but not everybody will do it. Some people are afraid to move out of their comfort zone, afraid to do something different. My message for them is: *"If you always do what you have always done, you will always be what you have always been"*. If you want to change the output, you have to change the input. The decision is entirely in your hands.

4

BUSINESS

"In business, sometimes, prospects may seem darkest when really they are on the turn. A little more persistence, a little more effort, and what seemed hopeless failure may turn to glorious success." - Elbert Hubbard

From the outside looking in, many people see salesmen and saleswomen as slick talkers who will go to almost any length to persuade the public to buy something they do not want. And they will often refer to selling as something people do while they are looking for a proper job. Inside a sales environment, however, things are, not unnaturally, viewed very differently. There, people will refer to selling as a good job, a great job, or perhaps even a tremendous career.

Personally, I do not subscribe to any of the above descriptions, from either side of the fence. Instead, I like to view selling as a business, and I view sales people as business people. My reason is very simple: selling is not just a job or a career, **it is a business!** Additionally, I believe that selling is the most important business in this country, or any other country.

Those people we mentioned who like to denigrate the salesman usually do so because they do not understand the importance of sales to a business. Frankly, with that kind of attitude, I have my doubts as to whether they understand anything at all about business. Ask them how they view the exploits of somebody like Henry Ford or John D Rockefeller. They will probably tell you how much they admired the success and the entrepreneurial spirit of these legendary figures. And if you asked them for a description of their activities, they would probably describe those pioneers as businessmen or innovators or entrepreneurs or almost anything other than salesmen. Yet Henry Ford did not become rich by producing cars, he became rich by selling cars. Equally, Rockefeller did not become the richest man in the world by discovering oil, he became the richest man by selling oil. Name any other millionaire or billionaire and the story will be the same. They did not acquire their wealth by manufacturing, or designing, or producing. They made their money by **selling** whatever it was that they manufactured, designed or produced.

Nothing happens in any business until a sale is made. And I do mean ANY business. It is not just the manufacturers who have to sell their products. Lawyers, doctors, banks, all have to sell their services if they want to remain in business. You, the sales person, are responsible for making that sale. It is you who is responsible for the success, the growth and the productivity of that business.

Perhaps we have to accept part of the blame ourselves for our none too professional image. After all, it is not unusual to hear sales people coyly refer to themselves as a consultant, a representative, an account executive, an associate or one of a dozen or more other equally contrived titles. It is as though they feel there is something wrong with proclaiming to the world that they are a salesman. How much better it is to stand tall and declare with pride *"I am a professional salesman"*.

There is also a valuable social aspect to our business. Whatever product or service you sell, you are responsible for the employment of numerous other people. After all, no company will employ people to produce a product or a service which they cannot sell, if they did, they would go out of business. So the next time you hear somebody attempt to denigrate the role of a salesman, ask them what they do, and then explain how a salesman keeps them in work.

We will return to the theme of the *professional salesman* throughout this book. As we do so I hope you will see it as more than a mere name, you should strive to make it an accurate description of your occupation.

5

COMMISSION

"Be delighted at the prospect of a new day, a fresh try, one more start, and perhaps, just perhaps, that special piece of magic waiting somewhere ahead." - J B Priestley

A former colleague of mine, a branch manager with a life assurance company, had some standard phraseology which he always used when interviewing potential agents. In explaining the difficulties of the job and the pay structure he would tell them: *"When things are going well, this is the best job in the world; but when things are going badly, it's the most painful way I know of going broke."* He was, of course, referring to the fact that in addition to being a tough business, the position was remunerated on a commission only basis. Commission is the most common method of pay in sales and one which evokes unusually strong feelings from people inside and outside the sales industry.

There are some salesmen who, given the choice, would shun commission for what they wrongly see as the security of a salary. For some totally illogical reason they seem to believe that it is only the commission earning salesman who has to make a sale in order to get paid.

Ask yourself, how many employers would be

content to pay a guaranteed income month after month to an employee who is not earning it? If a lathe operator is not producing the product, or the cleaner is not cleaning the offices, or the driver is not delivering the goods, do you suppose the employer would be happy to continue paying them? Of course not. Were he to do so, he would go out of business. It is no different for a salesman on a fixed income, when he is in a slump and not making the sales he becomes a drain on company resources. When this happens, he will very soon find himself looking for a new job.

Compare that with the salesman who is paid on commission. When he goes through a bad patch and fails to make the sale, then unlike his salaried colleague he does not cost the employer anything other than the normal overheads. Even so, he cannot be kept on for ever, but he is more likely to be given the opportunity to overcome his short term slump. For this reason, I believe the commission route offers more security than the salary which at first glance appears to provide a guaranteed income.

Accepting a fixed income also means that you have set a figure, and a limit, on your value. You are saying *"What you're prepared to pay me is all I'm worth"*, and when you put a small value on yourself, nobody else will raise the price. Commission means that you will always be paid what you are worth and the more you do, the more you get.

Not everybody would agree with those views however. You only have to read the newspapers to see how the outside world views commission. They see it as encouraging bad practices, again with the misguided belief that only salesmen on commission have to make a sale. They talk about the hard sell and commission hungry salesmen persuading people to buy things they neither want nor need. It is something of a paradox that many of those same people who denigrate the commission system, will applaud companies which involve their employees in profit sharing schemes. Those companies are commended for their forward thinking and their caring attitude. Yet, in reality, they are talking about the same thing.

When a product is sold, the price includes a mark up to cover costs and to provide a profit margin. Commission simply means you are paid part of this mark up when the sale is made; instant profit sharing. Being rewarded directly for your efforts is undoubtedly the fairest method of compensation that I know of.

6

COMMUNICATION

"In communication it is more important to get understanding than it is to get agreement." - Antoine de Saint-Exupery

I agree whole heartedly with the quotation above and would even go one step further by expanding it to say that when we do not get understanding, there will be no communication. It is a fact that the quality of your communication will determine the quality of your business. If you are unable to communicate clearly and effectively with your prospects it is unlikely that you will ever convert them to clients.

Make sure you hear what is being said. That sounds like obvious, straight forward common sense, and yet it is something that is often ignored in the sales situation. Sometimes without even realising it. Instead we make assumptions. We assume that our clients understand what it is we are saying to them. And even worse, we assume that we understand what they are saying to us. In other words, we assume that the message received is the same as the message sent, although research shows that half the time our assumptions are wrong. This means that neither party really knows what is being said.

The problem is that instead of listening, the

majority of people simply wait for their turn to speak. As a result of this, listening becomes passive rather than active. Put another way, this means that although they hear the words, they miss the message. Active listening changes this and we will look a little deeper at that aspect of communication in another chapter.

What about the words you use? Do you speak to people in their own language? I am not referring here to English or French or Spanish, but rather to the common, everyday language of those with whom we are communicating.

For communication, real communication, to take place you have to use words and phrases which are in common usage by your client or prospect. When you use language that is not familiar to them you will alienate them, and they will subconsciously turn off. Some of the worst examples of this can be heard from the mouths of pompous politicians. Many of these appear more intent on showing how many "big words" they know, than they do in communicating their message to the electorate. Perhaps they use it as a way of covering up the absence of a real message!

There are other politicians, of course, who are exactly the opposite and their communication skills are a joy to behold. American President John F Kennedy was a prime example. His skills were evident in every speech he gave. Sir Winston Churchill was another who could use the appropriate language at the appropriate time. It is interesting to note that both of those gentlemen rose to the top of the tree. Could their communication skills have had anything to do with that?

The same rules apply to the written word whether it is in a letter, a report, a fax, a brochure, an advertisement, or any other document you use in your business. If it cannot be understood by those it is aimed at, it will have very little effect. At least, it will have very little positive effect. It may well have a negative effect; it may well put people off dealing with you or your company. In my opinion, that is a risk not worth taking.

A good example of using the wrong language came from a lecturer who had been explaining the value of good communication skills. He proceeded to tell his audience that they should *"... help people to emancipate their thoughts"*. I am well aware that "Emancipate" means to free or to liberate, but it is not a word in common usage in that context so the lecturer lost his audience for a few minutes. The same person suggested in another part of his talk that you *"need to know where exactly the location you're searching is located"*. It took me a while to realise that he meant *"You need to know where you're going"*. In his efforts to impress us with his extensive vocabulary he confused the issue, alienated the audience and missed the message.

Why complicate things unnecessarily? The same rule applies whether it is oral or written, keep your communication clear and simple. As a general practice, your letters should never exceed one side of standard A4 paper. Do not make them any longer than this or you run the risk of losing your client's attention.

When you have a situation where, for instance, there are a lot of technical details you want to convey, refer to them in your letter but keep them on a separate sheet. Give your client the information in bite size chunks which he can readily assimilate. Far better to have a dozen neatly bound sheets, with each one uncluttered and detailing a different aspect of your product, than to have a two or three page letter crammed with information that is too much to take in all at once.

Remember, you are an expert on your product, your client may not be. Keep it simple and understandable. Avoid jargon at all costs; using it does not show how much you know, it shows how much you do not know.

7

DEVELOPMENT

"The purpose of learning is growth, and our minds, unlike our bodies, can continue growing as we continue to live." - Mortimer Adler

Development comes in two varieties, business and personal, but you cannot have one without the other. It is impossible to develop in one area of your life and stand still in another. In fact, going one step further, you really should not want to develop one area of your life more than another. When you attempt to do that you will throw everything into confusion. Although you may talk about your business life, your family life, your social life and so on, when it comes right down to it, they are all the same thing. Your life.

When you allocate, or attempt to allocate, your life into neat little segments you simply create problems for yourself. To which segment would you allocate a personal telephone call during business hours, or taking some work home with you one evening, or a night out in the company of business associates? It is the same with our development; our business development and our personal development should run hand in hand. When we grow as a businessman we will automatically grow as a person, and vice versa. When you learn to use a computer for business you will find it has a lot of applications in the home, when you learn to speak another language for your holidays you will find that your value on the job market has doubled, and so on.

Because I frequently give talks and run seminars on various aspects of personal development, I am often asked what is meant by development. I can answer that question simply and honestly in a number of ways: improvement, growth, maturity, knowledge, learning. Unfortunately, although those are all honest answers, they are not very helpful, for two reasons. Firstly, there is no single answer available because development is a combination of many things. Secondly, for most people that is not the question they meant to ask. A more meaningful question might well be *"What do I need to do and how do I plan my development programme?"*.

Simply by asking that question they have taken the first step. When you realise that you need to do something about your development, you have already started doing it. The next step, a little like goal setting, is to write a list, a list of improvements you would like to see in your life. Remembering what we have already said, these improvements can apply to any part of your life, not just your business. It might be that you want to gain more knowledge on a particular aspect of your business, start an exercise programme, learn to cook, read more, take an open university course, learn to paint, become an accomplished public speaker, etc. Whatever it is, write it down and do not stop until you have got everything on your list.

Now, spend some time studying your list, evaluating it and prioritising it. Is there anything missing, is there anything on there which should not be there? Which items are most important, most urgent, least important, which ones would it be practical to start today, do some rely on somebody else's time table? There will be a lot of questions to ask yourself before you are satisfied and at least one of those I can answer for you right now.

Question: *"When do I start?"* Answer: *"Today."* When you decide to leave it until tomorrow you will find that tomorrow never comes. And if you plan to start next Monday, you will find that when it arrives, next Monday turns into this Monday and next Monday is still a week away.

Be sure to make your programme varied. If it all goes in one direction it could become boring, and if it becomes boring you will not want to maintain it. Include items that are fun to do and items that involve other people. Attending seminars, training courses and conferences is one way of doing this. In this way you can learn from others and interact with other delegates, sharing common problems and experiences.

Check your programme and revise it from time to time. Development is not something you do for a month or two, or even a year or two; it is something you are involved in every day for the rest of your life. Informal things like reading a book, helping people with their problems, conversations and discussions will all aid your own development.

8

DREAMS

"I have learned this at least by my experiment: that if one advances confidently in the direction of his dreams, and endeavours to live the life which he has imagined, he will meet with a success unexpected in common hours." - Henry David Thoreau

If it really is true, as Walt Disney said, that all our dreams can come true if we have the courage to pursue them, why is it that we are still waiting to win the lottery? That seems like a reasonable question when you consider that Disney was not the only one of our illustrious predecessors to have told us time and again that if we can dream it, we can achieve it. So, what is the hold up? Why are we still waiting for the big win that we have dreamt about on numerous occasions? The answer is simple; the result is totally outside of our control.

As we saw earlier in this book, for something to happen we have to take action. Taking it a step further, that action has to be specific and has to lead us towards our dream. But equally important, there has to be the possibility that our action could lead to a successful outcome. In other words, it has to be possible - not definite, not even probable, just possible - for the outcome to be influenced in some way by some person or persons. With the lottery this is unfortunately not the case; numbers are chosen at random amidst strict security controls so we have absolutely no influence over the result.

To achieve our dreams therefore, we must pursue those which are achievable. For instance, if you are 18 years old and you dream of becoming an Olympic athlete, start training. It can be done. It does not matter that you may have no experience. The important thing is that such a dream could conceivably be realised. There are many stories to prove it, stories of athletes who went from nowhere to world class in a few short years. When you are 68 or 78, however, an Olympic dream would have very little chance of ever being fulfilled, not just by you, but by anybody. If it can be done by man it can be done by you, but if it cannot be done by anybody it will be fruitless pursuing it.

Incidentally, I am not suggesting for one moment that you should lower your sights and only aim for things which can be achieved with little or no effort. Far from it. After all, that which is gained without effort has little value. Aim higher. In fact, aim as high as you like and, bearing in mind what we said about possibilities, do not dismiss something just because it seems too difficult or too far away. The bigger the challenge, the more satisfied you will be when you overcome it. In that respect, I have always endeavoured to put into practice the words of George Bernard Shaw who said *"Some men see things as they are and say 'Why?'; I dream things that never were and say 'Why not?'."*

Your dream may be to become the top salesman in your industry, to open your own business, to learn another language, to become chairman of the company that employs you, to be a film star, to write a book, to obtain a degree, to have a specific amount of money invested, to be a top sportsman, to live in a different country, to own a particular car, to clear your debts, to work three days a week, or any one of a hundred thousand other things. Then do it. Whatever it is, if you want it badly enough, if your dream is real enough, and if it will not harm anybody else, you should go for it and ignore anybody who tries to dissuade you.

Do you remember Billy Payne? Back in 1986, Billy Payne was a 37 year old small time lawyer with a community spirit. He had organised church fetes and the like and raised the funds for an extension to his local church. Then he decided on his next project; to bring the Olympic games to his home town of Atlanta, Georgia. His wife was amongst those who, to put it mildly, expressed their doubts! But Billy was convinced he could do it. He gathered around him eight friends with similar church fete experience, instilled his dream in them and set off to convince the world.

During the ten years that followed he visited almost one hundred countries, gave thousands of major speeches, raised millions of dollars, and employed 3500 people. How could this happen? How could somebody whose previous experience was organising church fetes, convince the world that he was the man to organise the biggest and most important sporting event of the century?

It happened because Billy Payne believed he could make his dream come true, because his belief was totally unshakable and because he was prepared to take the necessary action to ensure others were aware of his belief and became equally convinced.

If Billy Payne can do it, you can do it.

9

EMPATHY

"How far you go in life depends on your being tender with the young, compassionate with the aged, sympathetic with the striving, and tolerant both of the weak and the strong. Because sometime in life you will have to be all of these".- George Washington Carver

Empathy is our ability to understand and to care about another person's feelings, the ability to put ourself in another person's place, to see things and consider our actions from their viewpoint. The North American indians referred to it as walking a mile in another man's moccasins. In our business, empathy is the quality which distinguishes the professional salesmen from the get rich quick merchants.

The professional salesman is not in business just for the money, any more than he is in business just for today. Of course he wants to make a sale like everyone else, and he wants to earn his money like everyone else. Contrary to what the press would have us believe however, he only wants to make the sale if it is right for the purchaser. The professional salesman is always looking long term and he knows a satisfied client will remain a client for many more years.

Anybody who treats a sales presentation like a

battle of wits, constantly attempting to get the upper hand and to win what he sees as a contest, will be very disappointed. He will be disappointed because he can never win. He is not alone, in such situations nobody can ever win. There may be a short term gain, but the long term loss will be far greater. An unhappy or dissatisfied client will never be good for business, for the salesman or his company.

In the best sales situations, where empathy is in evidence and where the salesman considers everything from the client's viewpoint, there is no contest and everybody wins. The product provider will sell one of their products, the salesman will earn his commission and, most importantly, the purchaser will get exactly what he wants.

The best way to ensure this happens every time is to spend the time necessary to build empathy with your clients, to get right inside their minds and find out what it is they really want. When you do this, your clients interests will always be at the forefront and you will automatically go out of your way to find the best way of providing what they want. There may well be times when this will result in a short term loss, but it will always result in a long term gain. A happy and satisfied client will come back to you time and again, and perhaps more importantly he will become a walking advertisement for you and your business.

There is no question that the time we spend on building empathy with our prospects and clients will be one of the best investments we ever make. When we build empathy we build a long term relationship. Dale Carnegie put it perfectly when he said *"We can make more friends in two months by becoming interested in other people, than we can in two years by trying to get them interested in us".*

So how do we go about it, what is the first step we need to take in the empathy building process? Talk to your client **about your client**, and listen to what he has to say.

Ask about his family, his business, his aspirations; anything to do with him. It will not require a great deal of effort on your part, people love to speak about themselves. You simply act in the same way as a chat show host, encouraging him to continue with his explanations and helping him out with a prompt from time to time.

The information you obtain will help you in helping him. You will know from the conversation whether he is in the market for your product or service. But do not look on it purely as a method of selling more. Your aim is to establish empathy which means taking a genuine interest in what he has to say. If you are unable to do this or if your personalities clash, thank him for his time and leave him for someone else. It will always be difficult to do business with somebody where there is no empathy or mutual respect. When you do show a genuine interest in what somebody has to say you will automatically establish empathy with that person and the business will follow.

10

ENTHUSIASM

"I studied the lives of great men and famous women, and I found that the men and women who got to the top were those who did the jobs they had in hand, with everything they had of energy and enthusiasm and hard work". - Harry S Truman

Enthusiasm is described in the dictionary as an *"ardent and lively interest or eagerness".* I like that. It is a good definition, and one which for me clearly and simply explains why successful people, in all fields of life, are always so enthusiastic about whatever they do. Study them, watch how they go about their daily business. You will see they do indeed have an ardent and lively interest in their chosen field, while their eagerness to succeed stands out like a beacon. They have discovered, like many others before them, that enthusiasm is the best paid quality on earth. If you want to emulate their success, make the same discovery and get paid accordingly. Your first step is to follow their lead.

The problem we face is knowing how to go about following that lead, how to go about building the kind of enthusiasm displayed by those we see as successful. There were no lessons on enthusiasm at my school and checking the prospectuses for the local colleges confirms that the education authorities are not providing any evening classes. This means that if you want it, you have got to do it yourself.

Many years ago I was told by a sales trainer that to be enthusiastic all I had to do was act enthusiastically. With no reason to doubt his wisdom, I decided to accept what he said and put it into practice. Incidentally, you may recognise that decision from something we said in an earlier part of the book, putting something into practice is called taking action! Surprise, surprise, it worked; just as he said it would. *"All the world's a stage and all the men and women on it merely players ... and one man in his time plays many parts"*. So whenever you are feeling a little less than enthusiastic, remember the words of both Shakespeare and my trainer, take centre stage, play your part and put on your act. You will soon appreciate, as I did, that when you act enthusiastically, it is impossible to feel anything but enthusiastic, and when you feel enthusiastic, you will become enthusiastic.

Follow that simple routine and you will know why enthusiasm is referred to as a miracle ingredient. It can change things instantly. The way you see things, the way you feel, the way you act, the way you go about your daily business, the way you interact with others, the way people see you. In fact, being enthusiastic will change your whole attitude to life. And amazingly, for this transformation to take place all you have to do is put on an act.

I know this all sounds almost too good to be true. After all, we are not accustomed to finding something so valuable so simple. We expect anything worthwhile to be either expensive or complicated, or both. The truth however is that it is neither of those; it is simple and it is free. But simple does not mean easy, simple just means simple. It still requires effort and persistence. When that effort and persistence are applied it works, and there is no question that enthusiasm really does make ordinary people extraordinary.

Perhaps the most wonderful thing of all about enthusiasm is that it is contagious. Be enthusiastic about your business and your enthusiasm will rub off on others like pollen on bees. And when you are both enthusiastic about the same thing the likelihood of doing business will increase one hundredfold.

11

FOLLOW UP

"The best preparation for tomorrow is to do today's work superbly well". - Sir William Osler

Ask an outsider what selling is, or what a salesman does, and he will invariably attempt to describe the sales interview, the time when the salesman and his client are together, face to face. But that is only a small part of the process. A little like an iceberg, that is the tip, the part the world sees. There is, however, a great deal more supporting the process that the world does not see.

Without support, and efficient back-up, there would be very little selling done. The problem is that very few salesmen have sufficient support staff to allow them to spend all their time face to face with clients. As a result they very often find themselves bogged down in the mire of administration and other unproductive activities. This chapter is part of a trilogy to get you out of that mire so that you can spend more of your time on the activities which are productive. The other two parts of the trilogy are in the chapters on Time Management and the Yellow Box Diary System.

I firmly believe that if you are going to do a job properly, you can only concentrate on one task at a time. In order to do this, you must have a clear desk. When there are papers lying around, haphazardly covering your desk, it is impossible to concentrate. Those papers get in the way, they remind you of other work which is waiting to be done, and they prevent you from thinking clearly about the task in hand. The first task, therefore, is to clear your desk, and keep it clear.

This is where the ten day follow up system comes in. It is a system which was first introduced to me when I joined the financial services business in 1978, and it has never let me down. Since then I have introduced the same system to hundreds of other businesses, of all types, where it has increased productivity on every occasion.

To operate the system all you need is an alphabetically indexed book, a bulldog clip, and a concertina file of the type you can buy in any stationers. They are usually advertised as home organisers and may well be indexed alphabetically, or chronologically. For our purposes, it does not matter how they are indexed because we are going to change it anyway.

You need thirteen sections in your file, ten for the follow up and three for the throw away. These should be labelled as follows:

- First ten sections numbered: 1 - 10
- 11: JANUARY APRIL JULY OCTOBER
- 12: FEBRUARY MAY AUGUST NOVEMBER
- 13: MARCH JUNE SEPTEMBER DECEMBER

Now start clearing your desk. First of all, have

you got any items that have been there for ages? Items that always get put to the bottom of the pile and never get done? If so perhaps they should be disposed of, thrown away. Before you decide that my suggestion sounds a little radical, think it through. How long have they been on your desk? A month, six weeks, two months? If they have been sitting around that long and nothing has happened as a result, are they really of any importance and are you ever going to do anything with them? What would be the consequences if you did nothing with them? Are you keeping them just so you can look busy when business is quiet?

If you are hesitant to dispose of them because you are not sure what the consequences would be, give them another three months. Use sections 11-13 in your file to put them away for three months. If you are clearing up in January file them under April, if you are doing the job in March file them under June, and so on. Make a note of them in your index book. You can index them by whatever reference you choose; the name of the client, the product, or anything else that is meaningful to you. Just write your reference for each item in your index book and beside them write "April", or "June", or wherever you have filed them.

This is the throw away section. When the papers reappear in three months time you will be in a position to make a positive decision on their fate. This is the section you use to file all those items you are not sure about. You can also use this section to write notes to yourself, reminding you of tasks to be done at that time. On the first working day of each month you remove everything from the relevant section. Delete them from your index book and go to work on them!

The main section, the follow up system, works in much the same way. When a piece of paper arrives on your desk or in your in-tray, decide what you want to do with it. Can it be delegated? If so, get rid of it immediately. If not, do you need to deal with it today? Could it be better dealt with tomorrow, or next week? If it has to be dealt with today, put it on your list, *see chapter on Time Management.*

If you are not dealing with it today, put it in the follow up system. If we assume that today is day one and you want to deal with it in five days time, put it in section number five. If today is day seven and you want it in five days time, file it in number two. Even if you are going to deal with it tomorrow, put it in your follow up and clear your desk. And, of course, enter everything in your index book in the way we described above. Each day take everything out of the appropriate section and deal with it.

You can use this same system when you are waiting for someone else to take action. For instance, if you write a letter and you expect a response within, say, eight days, put a copy of the letter in your file to be retrieved eight days later. If there has been no response in the meantime you know it is time to chase it up. During those eight days, however, you do not need to spend time thinking about it. If a response arrives before the eight days, you simply look at the reference in your index book and that will tell you where you have filed it.

The numbers on your file relate to working days only, ignore week ends and holidays. You may want to keep track of them by writing the numbers in your diary so you will always know what number any particular day is. An alternative to this is to put a bulldog clip on today's file and just move it on each day. Incidentally, if you find the concertina file is not big enough for your needs you can use a filing cabinet in exactly the same way. Just allocate the required number of files and give each one a number.

12

GOALS

"It is for us to pray not for tasks equal to our powers, but for powers equal to our tasks; to go forward with a great desire forever beating at the door of our hearts as we travel toward our distant goal".- Helen Keller

Over the years I have read numerous books, listened to dozens of tapes and attended many seminars on the subject of Goal Setting. Everybody, it seems, has their own proven way to set goals that work and it seems to me that the more you study it, the more confused you become. However, there is one thing on which they all appear to agree, by far the most important thing about goals is having one.

Just as you can never hit a target you cannot see, you can never reach a goal you have not set. That may seem like stating the obvious but the fact that it is obvious does not mean it is observed. Research has shown that one of the major reasons why people in business struggle is because they have no goals. If, therefore, you want to move on from your current situation, you must make a decision on how you want to progress, where you want to be at some point in the future.

Having done that, you have decided on what you would like your goal to be, but you have not set your goal. To do that you must write it down, in detail, together with a plan on how you intend to achieve it. If it is not detailed and in writing, it is not a goal. *"A house in the country"* is not a goal. A goal is *"A four bedroom stone built, georgian style house on a one acre site with a double garage, swimming pool and games room - by the end of next year".* A goal is specific.

Those who doubt the power of goals would do well to study the results of a survey carried out at Yale University in 1953. All students leaving Yale that year were asked to complete a questionnaire which asked them about their time at university and their plans for the future. When the papers were analysed it was discovered that only 10% of the students had any goals to take with them into the world of business. But, as we have already said, goals are not goals unless they are written, and just 4% of those surveyed had committed their goals to paper. In other words, only 4% had real goals.

As a research project in 1973, the university decided to trace those students of 20 years earlier and ask them to complete another questionnaire. The results were remarkable and confirmed what many people had been saying for years about written goals. Those results showed that, collectively, the 4% with written goals were worth more financially than the rest of the group put together who, two decades earlier, had left their studies with no clear picture of what they wanted from life.

Could this be because the 4% who had written down their goals knew exactly where they were going and steered their life in that direction, while the rest of the group allowed themselves to drift aimlessly like a ship without a rudder? I believe that is unquestionably the reason. If you want to achieve anything in life it is imperative that you define it clearly and commit it to paper.

Set goals that are within your control. If your goal is to be the number one salesman in your team, you could be on your way to a disappointment as you have no control over how other people in the team will perform and therefore your goal becomes unrealistic. It is much more realistic to set as your goal, a figure which you plan to achieve, a figure which under normal circumstances would make you number one. That way if another member of the team produces exceptionally high sales, it does not affect your goal.

You can control your own performance and your own activity and make plans accordingly, but you have no way of knowing whether somebody else has been making plans which are bigger than yours, or whether Lady Luck will show her hand in somebody's favour. Your aim should be to reach your own goal, to achieve the figures you planned, everything else is outside your control.

When Olympic athletes set their training programmes for the games four years hence, they are designed to achieve a certain time or distance. Of course, they want to win the gold but as a goal that would be too nebulous. A goal has to be specific, it has to be measurable and it must have a time frame. Our athletes set a specific time or distance they want to achieve for their event, they can measure their progress with intermediate events and they have a deadline set for them by the International Olympic Committee.

Follow their lead. Be specific. Ensure it is within your control. Set a time frame. Design a plan to achieve it. Commit it to paper. And then, most importantly, take action!

13

GROWTH

"If to grow is success, then one must wake up anew every morning and keep awake all day". - Henry Ford

Most people would agree that there are only three ways for a salesman to grow his business. The first, and perhaps the most obvious, is to acquire new clients and therefore enlarge his client base. The second way is to increase the average size of his sales which will result in higher production overall. The third is to increase the number of repeat sales or, in other words, to increase the number of sales he makes to his existing clients.

The first of those three is where we all begin. The self-employed salesman starts out with nothing and proceeds to build his business from scratch. Those who are employed, on the other hand, will often take over an existing territory with an established clientele. Should you find yourself in that position you will normally be given acquisition targets for new clients which you must achieve if you want to retain your job.

Acquiring new clients is not just for those who are new to the business, however. No business stands still and if your business is not growing, it is dying. Whichever category you fit into, employee or self-employed, it will be necessary throughout your career to find new clients in order to expand your business and to replace those you have lost through natural wastage.

Initially there is a temptation for everybody to go for numbers, to get the most clients in the shortest possible time. That is alright to start with but it is a recipe for disaster if you continue on the same track throughout your career. When you go for volume the quality will normally suffer, and with poor quality clients you will struggle to build a solid business. It is a fact in the sales business that the smallest clients usually create the biggest problems, and of course they also provide the lowest profits.

Having established your initial base, in order to build you must become more selective. Establish your own criteria that you want your clients to meet and then look specifically for clients who meet those standards. You do not necessarily have to increase the numbers, as you lose poor quality clients at the bottom end, replace them with better quality clients at the top.

Doing this will lead you into the second area of growth, increasing the average size of your sales. This does not involve browbeating your clients or pushing them to buy more than they want. The hard sell is for the cowboys, the professional salesman sells the client what he wants and what he needs. Better quality clients want and need more, or more expensive, products so automatically the average value of your sales will increase. Your productivity will also increase as you will find there is very little more work, or more expense, involved in making a large sale than there is in making a small sale. And, exactly opposite to what we said previously, the biggest clients usually create the smallest problems, and provide the highest profits.

It sounds very easy but like everything else, you have to work at it. Premier quality clients demand premier quality products, premier quality knowledge and premier quality service. Just like you, they have their own criteria for the people they want to deal with. If you cannot meet their standards you cannot expect them to do business with you. As a professional salesman you must make sure you are ready for a market before you enter it. That means study and research to improve your knowledge in that area.

The same criteria will determine whether you benefit from the third area of growth, increasing the number of sales to existing clients. Premier quality clients will generally be in a position to buy from you more often than those at the other end of the scale. But again, they will only do so if you can provide the kind of service they expect to receive. Sales is a service industry and if you are not providing a good service, you are not providing anything.

14

HABITS

"The wise man does no wrong in changing his habits with the times". - Dionysius Cato

We all have habits, some good, some bad. We also have a choice, we can accept our habits or change them. Habits are not something you were born with, and they are not permanent. They are learned behavioural responses to particular situations. So if you want to change a bad habit all you have to do is learn a new response and turn it into a good one. Some years ago Earl Nightingale suggested that if you changed the way you did something for thirty days it would become a habit. He was right, it really is as simple as that.

Bad habits in selling will invariably lead to bad results so it is important for us to find out what bad habits we have, and change them. This will not be an easy exercise, it is much easier to see someone else's bad habits than it is to see your own. For that reason I suggest you enlist the help of a colleague. Work together to identify each others habits and help each other to eliminate the bad ones and replace them with good ones.

Listen to each other on the telephone, do you smile, do you repeat yourself, do you use trite phrases or clichés, do you explain yourself clearly to the person on the other end? Go on sales appointments together, do you habitually use negative body language, do you listen, do you make assumptions? Make notes to help each other, are you always punctual, are you organised?

Take a look at how you present yourself, is there anything, anything at all, about your appearance which some people might find irritating, and which might distract their attention from your sales presentation. Something as simple as a tie that is not quite straight, or shoes that are not polished, or uncombed hair, or an untidy brief case. For one person such things may be of no importance whatsoever, but for another it could make the difference between making the sale or not. Why take the chance? Make it a habit to check your appearance before every meeting.

When things become habits they become easier. Do it first on something where the result can be easily measured, perhaps something as simple as getting out of bed in the morning. Very few people like getting up, it becomes a huge effort for them to drag themselves out of bed and as a result they spend their first hour or so feeling sorry for themselves as they drool into their coffee. Suggest to them that they get up even earlier and they will suggest to you that you are a few bananas short of a bunch!

Yet, in reality you will find it no more difficult getting up at 6.00 am than you would at 7.00 am, if you make it a habit. It might seem difficult at first but if you persevere for those thirty days it will become a habit and you will not even think twice about it. If all you do is get up an hour earlier, however, all that will happen is that you will feel sorry for yourself an hour earlier. So you have to change a few other habits at the same time.

Remember the little white cards we spoke about in the section on Belief? This is an ideal time to use them. Use phrases such as *"I get up at six o'clock every morning wide awake, full of enthusiasm and eager for work", "I smile as soon as I get out of bed", "Early morning is my favourite time of day".* Phrases like this will help you to change your attitude as well as your habits. Incidentally, an extra hour every working day will give you the equivalent of an extra four weeks of productive time each year. Could you do any extra business if you had an additional four weeks to do it?

If you are serious about improving your business and your life you must develop habits which will help you along that route. One final thing, reviewing your habits should become one of your habits.

15

HONESTY

"Five thousand years ago what I am saying was right. In five thousand years what I am saying will still be right: cleanliness, honesty, decency, respect for other people, politeness, good manners, integrity; they will never be old fashioned". - Lord Forte

To the best of my knowledge there is no product or service on the market today that will suit all the people all the time. This means that from time to time during the course of our business we will encounter somebody for whom our product or service is unsuitable. I am sure that this information comes as no major surprise to you, but what do you do in a situation like that? There could be numerous answers to that question but for the professional salesman there is only one, and that will come as no surprise to you either. You simply say *"Thank you for your time but it doesn't look as though I can be of any help to you today"*. You then leave and look for somebody who does need your services.

It sounds very simple although I can understand how there may well be times when following that procedure will cause you some difficulty, but nobody ever said this was an easy business. You may have gone to a lot of trouble, and expense, in finding your prospective client, you may have spent a good deal of time preparing for the meeting, you may have travelled for hours to get to the meeting, you may need the business to achieve your targets. There may be a hundred other reasons why you really want that business, all very valid reasons for feeling disconcerted at having to walk away from the sale. There are no valid reasons, however, for attempting to sell a client a product which you know is unsuitable for his requirements.

Losing a sale in those circumstances may be a big disappointment, but it is not a failure, it is a victory. A victory for honesty and professionalism and for the sales industry in general. The foundation for all success is integrity and honesty, and provided you can hold your hand on your heart and say those descriptions apply to you, you will achieve the success you deserve.

Mirabeau wrote many years ago that *"If honesty did not exist we should invent it as the best means of getting rich".* The only amendment I would make to that great man's statement is that we should invent it as the best way of doing business.

I recall a series of interviews I underwent prior to joining the financial services business. The interviews were being conducted by Peter Bassnett who had recruitment targets to meet, so bringing me into the business would have been a "sale" for him. Even so, he would not allow me to join until he had covered every possible aspect of the business, good and bad. He had to be satisfied in his own mind that I fully understood what the job involved and what could go wrong.

Peter told me that if I did join the business I would very soon find out exactly what it involved. If I was finding it tough or going through a bad patch, he did not want to be in a position where I could say *"You didn't tell me that".* He was a very tough manager, but was respected by everybody he worked with for his honest approach to the business. He was an excellent role model for the agents who worked with him and I am sure it is no coincidence that so many of them turned out to be top producers and managers.

Follow Peter's philosophy in your sales presentations. Whatever it is you are selling, the client will find out everything about it when he buys it. Make sure there are no surprises waiting for him by telling him ALL the facts before he buys it. A life assurance agent I once worked with told me that if you tell the truth often enough, sooner or later you will be found out. He was right, honesty is by far the best policy.

16

INTERVIEWS

"A tree as big around as you can reach starts with one small seed; a thousand mile journey starts with one small step". - Lao Tzu

The sales interview, or presentation, is where the theory stops and your knowledge gets put into practice. But that does not mean you should forget the theory, if you forget it you will be unable to put it into practice.

The first few minutes of any interview are the most important. It is during this time that your client will make an important decision about you, in just four or five minutes he will decide whether you and he are going to get on together, and therefore whether you and he will do business together. Hardly fair really, is it? After all, how can he know enough about you in such a short time to make such an important decision?

The answer is that perhaps he does not know enough. But that will not stop him making the decision. He will form an impression and make assumptions which will become part of his belief system. As a result, they will be extremely difficult, if not impossible, to change in the future. Before every client meeting, remind yourself of the old adage:

"You never get a second chance to make a good first impression".

How do you greet your prospect? Most people will say *"Good Morning"* or *"Good Afternoon"* and couple it with a handshake. That is fine, but to get a psychological advantage at the outset, you should be the one who offers his hand first, you can then compound this advantage by also being the one who speaks first.

A good firm handshake will show your client that you are sincere, other types of handshake can convey a completely different message, so make sure you handle this part of the interview right. If you get it wrong you could ruin everything in the first twenty seconds. Take note of how others shake hands with you and see how you feel in different situations. Your client is likely to feel the same way.

Someone who gives a weak handshake, like a wet lettuce, also gives the appearance of being nervous, weak and indecisive. Not really the sort of person who would inspire you to do business. At the other end of the scale is the crusher who holds your hand in a vice like grip until it turns white through lack of circulation. This macho type of person very often has an inferiority complex and tries to hide it with bravado of this nature. His attempts to show himself as friendly and sincere are lost in the pain! This is something most people would not want to perpetuate by doing business and having him call on a regular basis.

There are a number of other variations when it comes to shaking hands and the best thing I can say about them all is, avoid them. As in everything else, keep it simple and sincere.

Body language is vital in building rapport with your client, especially in those critical first few minutes, the handshake is just a part of it. Think about how you stand or sit when you are talking to your client. Do you stand over him and dominate him? If so he is unlikely to feel comfortable in your presence. Leave a reasonable space between the two of you so nobody feels threatened. Do you sit with your arms crossed? This forms a barrier between you and your client and makes it difficult to establish a relationship. Open arms show you have nothing to hide.

Do you maintain eye contact? On many occasions I have been in conversation with people while their eyes have stared into the distance as though they were unaware of my presence. I have also been on the receiving end of the person who closes their eyes while they are talking. I assure you, I did not enjoy either experience and I certainly would not do business with anybody who appears to be so ignorant.

This does not mean you have to stare into your clients eyes all the time, that will make them feel equally uncomfortable. Keeping eye contact around the area of the head and occasionally looking directly into their eyes will have the desired effect. As with so many other things it takes practice to get the balance right and much of it will be determined by your own intuition, by how you feel.

What do you call your client? Should it be "Bob", or "Mr Smith"? If you are not sure, ask him. *"Would you prefer me to call you Bob, or is it Mr Smith?"*. If he wants you to be on first name terms he will say so. On the other hand, if he says *"It doesn't matter"*, he means *"Call me Mr Smith"*.

What do you say? If you have trouble making small talk, spend some time before the appointment thinking of things to say which will be relevant to the client. If you are uncomfortable with this simply say to your client *"I realise you're a busy man so to save your time do you mind if we get straight down to business?"*. I have never yet known anybody to be upset by that opening gambit.

When there is nothing to say, you are better off saying nothing. Unlike a salesman who called on a friend of mine some years ago and insisted on continuing with unwelcome small talk even after my friend had made it perfectly clear that he did not have time to waste. The crowning glory came when the salesman noticed a painting on the office wall. In a miserable attempt to ingratiate himself with the client he proceeded to analyse the painting and show his expertise by giving a discourse on the merits of abstract art. Eventually he asked who the artist was and received the answer *"My eight year old daughter!"*. Needless to say, he left without the order.

17

INTRODUCTIONS

"There are no great men, only great challenges that ordinary men are forced by circumstances to meet". - Admiral William Halsey

The best way to meet a new potential client is to be introduced by an existing, satisfied, client. He can provide a third party endorsement on the quality of your product or service that will carry far more weight than anything you could possibly say about it. In the eyes of your prospect, your client has nothing to gain by recommending you, and that in itself is a very strong recommendation.

Everybody with more than twenty four hours sales experience knows that referrals are more effective than cold calling. Anybody who has not discovered this aspect of selling is in for a very short, or very unsuccessful, career!. Introductions take the process one step further.

The major difference is that when we ask for referrals, we say *"Who do you know that I could call?"* but when we ask for introductions we say *"Who do you know that YOU could call?"*. In other words, your client makes the initial contact. In doing this your client will automatically filter out those who have no interest in your product at that time so you will not have to waste your time, or theirs. On the other hand, he will prime those who would be happy to meet you so that when you get in touch with them, they are expecting your call.

How much easier do you suppose it would be to make an appointment with a prospect in those circumstances? How much more receptive to your presentation would the prospect be in those circumstances? How much more likely is it that the prospect would also be prepared to furnish you with introductions in those circumstances? Those are rhetorical questions, because you already know the answers!

So, if it is that much more effective why does everybody not do it all the time? The reasons are many. Some people are embarrassed to ask for names, either referrals or introductions, because they think it will upset the client. Some, having made the sale just want to get out as quickly as possible in case the client changes his mind. Some think it is an imposition and they have no right to ask. Some think the client will see it as unprofessional.

Provided you have done your job correctly, none of those reasons are valid. Firstly, you must have established a rapport with your client. Secondly, you must have done a professional job by providing him with a quality product or service. Finally, and perhaps most importantly, you have to ask in the correct manner. If you have done all three of these, there is only one reason why someone would be unable to furnish you with the required names when you ask.

When you are asking, remember that you are a salesman and this, in effect, is another sale to be made. Your client has not bought your product because it is the best of its kind, because it is cheap, because it will last a lifetime, because it looks good, because it sounds good, or because it is the latest model. He has bought it for one reason, and one reason only, because there is a benefit to him in doing so.

If he is to provide us with referrals or introductions, there must also be a benefit to him in doing so, and the benefit should be explained when we ask for his help. But before we look at the benefit to the client we need to go back a step. I said there was only one reason why he would be unable (please note: unable, not unwilling) to furnish the required names. The reason is that you have taken him by surprise and he is unable to think of any on the spur of the moment, or he is unsure about the type of person you want to meet.

The best way to overcome this is to mention introductions at the start of your presentation, as soon as you meet the prospect. *"Mr Prospect, as you know I'm here today because of Mr Client's recommendation. I find this is the most professional way of meeting new clients - through introductions from my existing clients and others I meet in the course of my business. I'd like to ask for your help in this area before I go today but before we do that, I'd like to see how I can be of assistance to you".*

You have broken the ice and primed him for the request you will be making later, after you have demonstrated to him that you deserve his help. You have also made it easier for him as he does not have to think of the names immediately. Subconsciously, however, he will be thinking of them throughout your presentation so he will be able to bring them to mind when you do ask him.

But what is the benefit to the client in providing the names to help you? There are two benefits. Firstly, he will be able to help his friends and colleagues by introducing them to a professional. In fact, provided you can demonstrate that your product or service is everything you say it is, he would be doing his friends a disservice by not introducing you. And surely he would not want to miss an opportunity to help them.

The second benefit to him is that it will allow you to continually provide him with a first class service, and you can explain this to him in just a few sentences. *"Mr Client, most people in my business spend 80% of their time looking for new clients which leaves them with just 20% to provide a service for their existing clients. I prefer to turn this around and spend 20% of my time contacting new clients and the remaining 80% looking after my existing clients, like you. That way I can continue to provide you with a first class service. In order to do this, however, I do need your help .....".*

When you are looking for people of a specific type, let him know so he can focus on those who meet your criteria. *"Mr Client, I'm looking for people who own their own business"*, or *"Mr Client, I'm looking for people in a similar job to yourself with other companies"*, or *"Mr Client I'm looking for ....".* You know who you want to meet, help your client to help you by pointing him in the right direction.

When you want to expand your market quickly in a particular area, use manufactured introductions. This will take all the pressure off your client as he no longer has to think of who to recommend. Make up a list of companies you would like to deal with and then, before you 'phone them out of the blue, take the list with you when you visit clients or prospects in the same type of business or in the same geographical area. Show them the list and say *"Mr Client/Mr Prospect, I'm going to contact all these companies shortly. Tell me, do you know any of them?".* He will proceed to qualify the names for you, telling you who he does or does not know. If you are simply asking for referrals, as opposed to introductions, you then say *"When I call them, do you mind if I mention your name and let them know that I deal with you?".* Again, if you have done your job properly he is very unlikely to refuse.

To turn a referral into an introduction, simply ask your client: *"Would you mind giving him a call now and letting him know I'll be contacting him?".* The best ideas are often the simplest, and this is no exception.

18

JOINT WORK

"Advice is seldom welcome; and those who want it most always like it the least". - Earl of Chesterfield

Joint work can be a shortcut to the top for the new salesman and a stimulus for the experienced salesman.

In the early part of our careers we will often come across opportunities which, quite simply, we cannot handle for one reason or another. It could be an area where we have little experience, in fact we may not even know what the opportunity is, we just know from our conversations with the client that there is something there.

I recall during my early days in financial services meeting clients who had estate planning problems or investment concerns that were way beyond my knowledge at that time. My choices were clear. I could walk away and leave it or I could attempt to fumble my way through it. But neither of those methods would have produced what I wanted, business on the books and a satisfied client. My alternative route , and the one I took, was to invite a more experienced colleague to work jointly on the case. This way not only did I secure the business but I was able to enjoy the very best kind of on the job training by watching an expert at work.

Some salesmen find it hard to come to terms with splitting whatever income the business may generate. Instead, they attempt to fumble their way through to what invariably ends up with an unsatisfactory conclusion where there is no benefit for the salesman or his client. Perhaps they feel they are giving away what they perceive as their money. But at that point there is no money, money is the result of completing the business successfully and attempting to fumble your way through something is not the best way of achieving that result. Never look at it as giving away income, think of it instead as investing in an education which will repay you many times over in the future. Forget any short term losses and consider the long term advantages of having a satisfied client, and remember that 50% of something is always worth more than 100% of nothing!

Some may feel it makes them look incompetent because they have to bring somebody else in to handle specialised areas of the business. Nothing could be further from the truth. If your ultimate aim is to provide the client with the best possible solution to his problems, then utilising the talent around you is the professional way of working. If that is not your ultimate aim, find a new job.

When you have a medical problem you go to see your General Practitioner. If he feels you need the attention of a specialist he will not hesitate to recommend that you see one. He will not be embarrassed by passing this specialised area of his business on to somebody better qualified. His ultimate aim is his patients well being and he will make use of all the talent at his disposal to achieve that aim. When it comes to dealing with complicated legal problems, a solicitor will very often consult another solicitor with specialised knowledge, or perhaps instruct a barrister. That does not mean he is incompetent. Just the opposite, it shows him to be thoroughly professional with his clients interests at the forefront. If it is good enough for those professionals, it is good enough for me.

What about the other side of the coin, what is in it for the experienced salesman who gives up his time to work with the newcomer? The answers are exactly the same. Business, income and education. Again, 50% of something is worth more than 100% of nothing. Remember always that this is extra, over and above your normal business. This is income you would not otherwise have generated. Because you are sharing it with somebody else and therefore will only receive half of the commission you may feel it is unprofitable. But remember, there is no marketing or prospecting involved, the groundwork has been done, much of the information you need has been collected and you have somebody else to collect whatever else you feel is necessary. When you consider all these points, you will appreciate that it can often be a very profitable way to work.

The profits are more than just financial, they are also educational. Working with another salesman is a great way to improve your own knowledge. It is amazing how sharp you become when we know you are being observed in minute detail. Do it, and everybody will benefit.

19

KNOWLEDGE

"Just as the bee gathers honey from all flowers, so the wise man gathers knowledge from all men". - Indian Proverb

KISS and KASH are two mnemonics which you are certain to encounter at various points in your career and two which contain all the ingredients you need for a successful career in sales. Having acquired and developed the **K**nowledge **A**ttitude **S**kills and **H**abits of KASH you only have to **K**eep **I**t **S**imple and **S**incere (KISS) to guarantee your success.

Attitude and Habits have been covered earlier in this book and we will be talking about Skills in another chapter so, for the time being, that leaves us with Knowledge.

Not only is it desirable to improve your knowledge, but in today's environment it is essential. How do you identify potential clients if you have no knowledge of the market place? How do you satisfy a client's needs if you do not know what those needs are? How do you know if your product will do the job if you do not know what the product does or what the job is?

Knowledge is not an option, it is essential for anybody who is serious about selling. Your clients expect it and deserve it, and in many cases regulators demand it. But that in itself is not a good reason for acquiring knowledge. Wanting to do the job in a professional manner is a good reason. Wanting to help your clients, and establish the empathy we mentioned earlier in the book, is a good reason.

It is often said that knowledge is power but I disagree, I believe that knowledge is only **potential** power. The decisive factor is how you use your knowledge, and this is where KISS comes in. The old maxim that says *"Clients don't care how much you know until they know how much you care"* has been around for a very long time. There must be a reason why it has stood the test of time, a reason why so many sales trainers repeat it in their training sessions. I believe that reason is very simple, it is true. There are many ways to show your clients how much you care, they are all important but none more so than the application of knowledge.

You will find countless opportunities to put your knowledge to use. For instance, you could show your clients just how much you know, and how clever you are, by explaining every possible intricacy of the product, and by demonstrating your knowledge of the technical jargon using a concept known as *blinding them with science!* The only problem with that approach is that is does not work and it does not help anybody. You simply end up confusing your clients, and no matter how slick your presentation was, you are hardly likely to do business with someone who does not understand what you were talking about.

Lin Yutang said: *"The wisdom of life consists in the elimination of non-essentials."* In part this means you should use your knowledge to eliminate the jargon and translate the technical aspects of your product into layman's language your client will understand. For example in the financial services business I have yet to meet a client who has expressed an interest in a scheme approved under Chapter IV part XIV of ICTA 1988; but I have met many who are interested in discussing how a Personal Pension could be used to provide them with an income in their retirement.

What this means of course is that you have to study, and you have already started that process by reading this book. Now continue the process with a combination of formal and informal study. Of course, you must do whatever is necessary to acquire the specific product knowledge required to assist your client in his deliberations, but look at other areas as well. Do you need to improve your presentation or public speaking skills, do you practice active listening, what do you know about your clients business problems?

Look for opportunities to improve your knowledge in every area. Read books, listen to tapes, attend seminars, ask questions, and listen to others. And one final point: do not treat your studies as an imposition, enjoy them and I know you will enjoy and benefit from the knowledge they bring.

20

LIMITING BELIEFS

"I believe that anyone can conquer fear by doing the things he fears to do, provided he keeps doing them until he gets a record of successful experiences behind him". - Eleanor Roosevelt

A limiting belief is a barrier, a psychological barrier that is stronger and more durable than almost any physical barrier you will encounter on your journey through life. And yet, such a belief has no foundation, no substance, and no logical reason for existence.

Limiting beliefs hold you back and prevent you from achieving the things in life which you know you are capable of. In sales they prevent you from moving up market by telling you that you are not good enough, you have insufficient experience, knowledge, talent or skill. They convince you of a myriad of nonsensical ideas such as telling you somebody else does more business because they are better than you, or older than you, or younger than you, or a hundred other things, all equally ridiculous.

Limiting beliefs tell you that you cannot stop smoking, you cannot lose weight, you cannot move out of your comfort zone and a host of other things that you cannot do, related to both your personal and business life. But if you want to succeed in life you have to remember that success comes in cans, not in cannots and therefore you have to get those limiting beliefs out of your life.

Take smoking as an example. I am a subscriber to Dr John Tickell's view that it is impossible to be intelligent and smoke at the same time. I do realise, however, that there are many people who disagree with that statement because they believe they are addicted and are therefore unable to stop. That is a limiting belief, and it is just as ridiculous as any of the others we have already mentioned. Of course you are not addicted, and there is nothing to prevent you quitting except your own limiting beliefs. If a smoker **wants** to stop, I firmly believe he or she can do so with very little fuss or bother.

Again I agree with Dr Tickell who says the way to stop is *"... don't put any more in your face".* (Dr Tickell is Australian and that is his Aussie talk for *"Don't light any more".)*

Perhaps that solution sounds too simple, but only to those who choose to believe it should be difficult. And some people do choose that, because they want to believe it is difficult and fraught with problems. They do not want to stop, but they want someone else, or something else, to take the blame. If they admitted that it really is as easy as I am saying it is, they would have no excuse for continuing to smoke. Sorry to disappoint them, but the truth is that it is that easy.

If you genuinely want to stop, you simply make a decision to become a non-smoker and then *"don't put any more in your face"!*

But what about all the trauma, the withdrawal symptoms, the frayed nerves, the bad temper, and all the other things we hear about? They are limiting beliefs and they do not exist; unless you want them to exist, unless you want to continue the illusion that you are incapable of making your own decisions. I have often wondered if the myth that says it is difficult to stop smoking is perpetuated by the tobacco companies as a way of maintaining their sales.

What gives me the right to make this claim, and to go against the popularly held beliefs and the writings of the tabloid journalists? Experience. First hand experience. I used to smoke 60 cigarettes a day until I decided to become a non-smoker. The transition took me less than twenty four hours and the only difficult thing was getting used to walking past the tobacco shop instead of calling in to waste my money.

It is exactly the same in selling, or in any other area of your life. If limiting beliefs are preventing you from moving forward, get rid of them and take control of your life. Install positive beliefs to replace them. One good way of doing this is by using the affirmation cards we mentioned in the chapter on beliefs.

Decide what it is you would prefer to believe and use that belief as your positive statement. Remember, it must be written in the present tense, as though you have already achieved it. Limiting beliefs are like habits, they can be changed, if you want to change them.

Many life long salesmen believe their knowledge is falling behind, or that they are struggling to keep pace with the new technology, or that they are being usurped by new, younger and more dynamic recruits. At the same time, those more recent recruits to the business often feel they lack the experience and maturity to deal with particular clients, or that they lack the in depth knowledge of the products that will allow them to break into new markets. As a result of these limiting beliefs, neither group performs to the best of their ability.

Using the affirmation cards they could change their beliefs by majoring on their strengths, and turning perceived weaknesses into further strengths. Look at a perceived weakness, analyse it and discover what it is that makes you believe it is a weakness. What would you need to believe in order to convert that perceived weakness to a strength? When you have the answer to that question, you have the statement for your card and you have the solution to help you move forward.

As an example, "I'm too old" could translate to "My experience gives me an advantage over my competitors". "I'm too young" might become "My energy and enthusiasm enable me to overcome all problems". You can think of dozens that will apply to your own situation. Just remember that limiting beliefs are not real, and they are not permanent.

21

LISTENING

"Nature has given to men one tongue, but two ears, that we may hear from others twice as much as we speak". - Epictetus

It is often said that we have two ears and one mouth, and should use them in the same proportion. Often said, but rarely done. As we said in the chapter on communication, instead of listening, the majority of people simply wait for their turn to speak. They stand like a tiger, waiting for the opportunity to pounce as soon as a gap appears in the conversation. And because they are so busy looking for the gap they fail to hear what is being said.

That may be all very well for cocktail parties and the like where the words seldom contain a message, and where idle conversation is commonplace. But it has no place in business where the aim should be to turn conversation into communication. That means making it a two way affair where you understand everything that is being said and just as importantly, or perhaps even more importantly, where you understand everything that is not being said.

Communication is more than just words and active listening entails using your eyes as well as your ears. The emotion behind the words, inflection, volume, facial expressions, eye movements, gestures, they all play their part in telling you what the speaker is attempting to communicate. Miss any of these subtleties and you miss an important part of what is being said, miss what is being said and you fail to establish dialogue, fail to establish dialogue and your chances of doing business are reduced to virtually nil. It is a constant circle and the only way to break out of it is by listening, active listening.

You must give your full attention to the speaker instead of using his speaking time as rehearsal time for your response. Establish eye contact, watch his gestures and listen carefully to the emphasis he puts on his words or phrases. Where the emphasis is placed is just as important as the kind of emphasis. Even a slight change of emphasis can change the whole meaning of what is being said. A prime example of this is the simple sentence *"Do cats eat rats?"*. Just four words but, depending on which word you emphasise, it can give four different meanings to the same question. If there can be such ambiguity with just four words, imagine what could happen in an hour long conversation or presentation.

So how do we avoid such ambiguity, how can we be sure that what we thought we heard is what the speaker thought he said? The answer is to use a simple, tried, tested and totally reliable formula: *If in doubt, ask!* Ask for clarification, for confirmation, for elaboration, and for anything else that is needed until we are confident that we understand the message beyond all doubt.

People are often afraid to ask because they feel it gives the impression that they have not been listening. Nothing could be further from the truth. By asking we are showing the speaker not only that we have been listening, but that we are interested in what he has to say and that we place sufficient importance on it to want to fully understand it. It is quite possible to ask without interrupting his chain of thought.

Open questions which require more than a "Yes" or "No" answer are probably the simplest, and certainly the most effective, way of asking. Such questions as *"Could you just clarify the point about ....",* or *"Would you mind going over that part again ....",* or *"That's very interesting, but I don't think I totally understand ..."* etc. Questions of this nature are rarely even seen as questions but rather as expressions of interest, and when you express interest in what someone has to say they will be more than happy to repeat or re-phrase their comments.

When you think you understand what the speaker thinks he said you should paraphrase the information and feed it back to him for confirmation that you have got it right before you act on it. *"As I understand it, what you're saying is ..."* or *"Just to make sure I haven't misunderstood ..."* or *"Let me just see if I've heard you right ..."* or even *"Do you mean ...".* Again you are showing your interest and again they will be happy to confirm whether you have got it right or not.

Obtaining clarification will never be a problem, when somebody is telling you about themselves or their plans, there is nothing they like more than an eager audience and the opportunity to keep talking.

Remember, a conversation is not a contest, it is not necessary to win every point. In any situation, but particularly in business, it is far more important to understand the other person's point of view than it is to win an argument. There is nothing to be gained by winning the battle if you end up losing the war, or the sale!

You may not get it right first time, or every time. Your mind may wander as you revert to your old habits and start rehearsing your answers or start looking for a way to jump in before the other person finishes speaking. Like everything else, however, if you work at it you will improve. Listening is a skill and like all the other skills you learn in life, practice makes perfect.

22

MARKETING

"I have stood on the shores of time picking up a beautiful seashell here and there while all before me lies the great sea of life, undiscovered". - Sir Isaac Newton

Marketing is not something you leave to the marketing department, marketing is something personal to you, the salesman. Of course the company will carry out research and make sure there is a potential market for the product before sending the salesman out to sell it. But where do you go, who do you talk to, what do you tell them, what are the benefits to the client? These, and many more, are questions we have to ask, and to answer, as part of our own marketing.

Keith Carby, the former Managing Director of J. Rothschild Assurance, described marketing for salesmen as *"ways of making sure as much of your working day as possible is spent seeing people who have a need for your services and are capable of paying for those services".* It is an excellent description and becomes even more meaningful when you realise it breaks down into four of the constituent parts of marketing:

Planning	Ways of making sure as much of
Time Management	your working day as possible is spent
Targeting	seeing people who have a need for your
Productivity	services and are capable of paying ....

If you take heed of Keith's description and spend your working day in the way he suggests, your marketing will be taken care of. As always, however, there is a little more to it than at first meets the eye. Your first course of action in developing your marketing plan should be to set some objectives. These will vary depending on your product, your current methods of marketing, back up from your company, etc. A few examples might be to create a 12 month marketing plan, to monitor the success of your plan, to engineer a change of direction or to introduce a "Minor Risk" strategy.

The minor risk strategy is where you test the water before jumping in. If the way you are working now is producing results which are acceptable it would be foolish to change everything overnight. Squeeze what you are doing now into three or four days and spend the newly released time on your new markets. If that is not possible, then drop some of what you are doing now in favour of a new approach. You have to be prepared to change, but do not risk everything without your own, practical, market research.

Start with the "Broad Concept" principle which consists of four questions:

1 Where am I now?

2 Where do I want to be?

3 What ways are there of achieving it?

4 Which is the best way for me, right now?

Question one will be answered by your records which we will look at in detail later in this book. What are your current targets, your level of sales, your markets, your acceptance by clients?

Question two is very personal, and you are the only person who can answer it. In an ideal world how would you like your business to change, what markets do you want to get into, what increase would you like to see in your sales? What would you consider to be the pinnacle of success?

Question three requires some lateral thinking. Is there more than one way to achieve these goals? Get out a pad and start writing. Commit to paper every possible way there could be to get to where you want to go. Do not evaluate your thoughts, just write down everything that comes into your mind. Some of the things you write may appear absurd at the time but that does not matter. If you attempt to rationalise things in your mind you will restrict your thoughts. Just write anything that might be possible, not only things which you believe you are capable of.

When, eventually, you have exhausted every possible route, sit back and look at what you have written. This is the time for evaluation. This is the time when you decide which route will be the best, the most productive, for you. Do not restrict yourself to what has gone before, the past does not equal the future and you are making a fresh start.

The quality of your marketing will determine the

quality of your business so do not rush this job. Invest the time such an important aspect of your business deserves. And having decided on your marketing plan do not stop there. Marketing is a permanent part of your business which means you must constantly be revising and updating your strategy.

23

MOTIVATION

"The only person we are accountable to is the one we see in the mirror every morning; that is the only one who knows if we have given it 100%". - Brendan F Power

Motivation is something everybody looks for but it is something most people have trouble finding; mainly because they spend much of their time looking in the wrong place. They look in the wrong place because they are looking for somebody else who will provide that motivation for them. That is not the way it works. You are the only person who can motivate you. Nobody else can do it for you, motivation has to come from within. I am sure you have heard those ten little two letter words which sum it up admirably: *"If it is to be it is up to me"*.

Well, if that is the case, why should you bother listening to motivational speakers, attending seminars, reading books, listening to tapes and so on? After all, if they are not going to provide the motivation you are looking for, you may well feel that you are wasting your time. And that would not be an unreasonable conclusion for somebody who does not know the full story. When you do know the full story, however, you will know that activities such as those above are never wasted.

What we are getting at here is that although none of those outside sources will motivate you, they will provide you with the stimulation to help you find your own motivation to drive you forward. In other words, they will encourage you to take action and to do something for yourself, and that is why they are invaluable to you.

"So where do I go from here, how do I motivate myself?". An easy straight forward question, but unfortunately I am unable to provide you with an equally easy and straight forward answer. That is because we all motivate ourselves differently, and we are all motivated for different reasons. The two overriding keys to motivation however are pain and pleasure. One person will be motivated by the thought of achieving success while his companion will be equally motivated by the thought of avoiding failure.

When you discover for yourself which one works best for you, pain or pleasure, you will be in a position to provide all the motivation you need to inspire yourself to action. It is not difficult to make the discovery but it does require action and effort on your part. On a number of occasions in this book I ask you to think. To think about something in your current behaviour, or to think back to a previous incident, or to think about where you want to go. These are not just throwaway lines. Thinking is a very important part of your development and your success. Henry Ford once said that *"Thinking is the hardest work there is, and that is why so few people engage in it".* I agree with him.

Just think back to a time when you were really motivated to do something, anything. Take your time and think carefully, this is a valuable exercise and you need to get it right. If you attempt to motivate yourself for the wrong reasons it will not work and you will end up being frustrated, so a few minutes now will be time well invested.

Think about it. Was your motivation the glory at the other end, the plaudits, the recognition, the applause, the admiration of your peers? Or were you motivated by the thought of the pain you would suffer if you failed, perhaps by having to watch somebody else receive the recognition and admiration while you are treated like an also ran? Incidentally, it does not matter which camp you fall into, each one is equally motivational, with the right people.

It is a good idea to reward yourself when you achieve your goals, and let the reward itself become the motivation. These rewards can be large or small just as the goals can be large or small. A cup of coffee when you have made 10 or 20 or 30 telephone calls, a meal at your favourite restaurant when you beat last month's figures, a weekend away when you are 10%, or 15% or 20% ahead of your target, etc. You choose the goals, you choose the rewards, the only rule is that they must be meaningful to you in some way.

Work with a colleague if you find this more effective. Help provide the stimulus for each other's motivation. Perhaps the first one who makes the required number of 'phone calls, or appointments, or whatever, gets the coffee bought by the other one. Or the one with the lowest figures at the end of the month has to buy dinner. Make it fun, and again the only rule is that the goals, the targets and the rewards are meaningful to you, it does not matter whether the same thing would motivate someone else.

24

NEURO LINGUISTIC PROGRAMMING

"The growth of the human mind is still high adventure, in many ways the highest adventure of all". - Norman Cousins

Neuro Linguistic Programming, or NLP as it is more commonly known, was introduced to the world during the 1970's by Richard Bandler and John Grinder in their book *"Frogs Into Princes"*. The book was really an academic report, but in recent years NLP has lost much of its academic bias in favour of more practical applications. Many of these applications are particularly useful to us as salesmen.

Most forward thinking sales trainers now incorporate elements of NLP in their programmes and in my own seminars I am constantly asked for more information on this comparatively new technology. Many sales people see it as the saviour they have been looking for - the so called "secret of success". And it can be, with one proviso. You have to combine the three letters of NLP with the four letters of WORK!

NLP will make your work more effective and more productive by providing you with new techniques but it will not do the job for you. For instance, one important element of NLP divides people into three basic groups, depending on how they access information: visually, auditory or kinaesthetically (emotions or feelings). It then teaches you simple ways to recognise which group an individual is in by watching his eye movements. When an individual is asked a question which requires a little bit of thought he moves his eyes in a particular direction before answering.

Looking up, towards the forehead, signifies looking into the memory for a picture to help them with the answer. These people obviously access information visually. Looking from side to side, at your ears, means you go through auditory or sound information for your answer. Those who access their information kinaesthetically will look downwards, towards their chin, for their inspiration. This is, of course, just the very basics of the process and there is a lot more to learn.

Learn it, it is worth the effort. Imagine how much easier the sales process would be if you knew which of those categories your clients were in. It would allow you to tailor your presentation specifically in a way you know will appeal to him.

You can build in language which you know will arouse his interest.

With a visual, you can *"show"* him your product, *"point out"* the advantages, *"take a look"* at the benefits and so on. These expressions would have very little effect on an auditory however. He would respond better when you *"ask"* him how he likes the *"sound"* of something or when you *"talk"* him through the benefits. For a kinaesthetic you need to change again in order to determine how he *"feels"* about the product, or if he has got a *"grasp"* of the benefits, or if he understands what a *"solid"* proposition it is.

Another technique which is very effective in the

sales process is *"Mirroring and Matching".* With a little practice, this will enable you to quickly establish rapport with your client by closely matching his demeanour and his voice style. This does not involve becoming an impersonator! It simply means listening to his tone and the pace of his voice, and matching it.

If he speaks slowly, slow your speech down to get closer to his pace. If his speech is more akin to a rapid fire machine gun, you might need to speed up a little. You may not feel comfortable going as fast as him, and you do not have to. It is not necessary to be identical, but is important not to be the opposite. Incidentally, it is very important that in doing this you do not end up sounding unnatural.

Apply the same thinking to your body position. Note your client's deportment and casually copy it. Again, it does not have to be identical. Sit or stand with a similar posture, mirroring some of his actions. Are his legs crossed, are his arms on the desk, are his hands clasped? Matching his actions in this way will make him feel more relaxed in your company and consequently more likely to do business with you.

As you know, the aim of this book is to introduce you to some of the key elements of success in selling. Clearly the space does not exist here to cover in detail such a multifarious topic but with numerous books, tapes and training courses now available on the subject and I would strongly recommend you to find out more about it.

25

NOTES

"There are two kinds of genius; those who are born a genius, and those who take notes". - Peter Bassnett

The next time you attend a conference, a seminar, or a sales meeting, have a look around you and see how many people are taking notes. And perhaps more importantly, see how many people are not. I am constantly surprised whenever I carry out this simple exercise and I always end up asking myself the same question. Why? Why would somebody take the time and trouble to attend the meeting if they do not have sufficient interest to take notes?

To me it seems such a waste of their time to sit watching a speaker or trainer imparting valuable information and then allowing it to just drift by. Although, maybe I misjudge them, perhaps unlike the rest of us they have an unfailing and super-retentive memory. But if that is not the case, and frankly I would be amazed if it was, how can they gain any benefit from what has been said if they do not take notes? How can they expect to put that knowledge to use if they cannot remember what has been said?

I firmly believe that the best advice anybody can give you is to take as many notes as possible. One word of warning however, be careful not to miss the talk as a result. If you are not alert to the problem, you can become so engrossed in your writing that you miss vital elements of the talk. The only solution to this is practice, if you take notes regularly you will soon develop the habit of listening and writing at the same time.

Having taken the notes what do you do with them? Please do not emulate one person I knew who meticulously filed his notes away in a filing cabinet, neatly labelled in subject order where they could be accessed at any time. When I asked him when the last time was that he had made use of the treasure trove of information stored away in his cabinet, he was more than a little embarrassed to answer *"I can't remember"*.

What a terrible waste of time, energy, resources and knowledge. There is absolutely no point in having your notes easily accessible if you do not take the time to access them. In fact, if you are not going to use them there is no purpose in taking notes in the first place. It would be a pointless exercise and a waste of your valuable time.

Mark Twain must have had something like this in mind when he said *"The man who does not read good books has no advantage over the man who cannot read good books"*. Reading and writing are two of the most valuable skills we will ever acquire, we should use them whenever possible.

Fortunately, there is a very simple, tried and tested method of utilising your notes and making sure they work for you over and over again. As soon as possible after you have taken the notes, and while the details are still fresh in your mind, review them. Go through them carefully and look for the items which you feel are particularly important to you. Highlight those items and then pick out the salient points. The next step is to re-write them on to index cards which you keep in an open file box on your desk.

It is important that the file box is kept open if you are to avoid falling into the *"out of sight out of mind"* trap, like my friend with the filing cabinet. All you have to do now is get into the habit of reading them regularly. Invest five or six minutes every day. Read one card and then put it at the back of the box, read another and put that at the back, and so on.

You can use the cards for technical information, inspirational quotes or anything else that you feel will be of benefit to you. It is not important for the information to be of any interest or any relevance to anybody else. This is your pool of knowledge which will provide you with a constantly changing source of specially selected positive material, specially selected for you, by you.

26

OPPORTUNITIES

"The pessimist sees difficulty in every opportunity, the optimist sees opportunity in every difficulty".- Sir Winston Churchill

Opportunities are there, all around us, everywhere we go and everywhere we look. Even so, they are not always easy to recognise because there are no labels on them and nobody will point them out to us. In fact, it is far more likely that they will arrive in disguise, disguised as misfortunes, obstacles, or problems or difficulties. A guaranteed route to success is to turn those obstacles into opportunities. To do this you have to see through the disguise, recognise them for what they are, and act on them before they disappear. You may be sure that if you do not take the initiative others will, and they will succeed in your place by seizing those opportunities you have ignored. No opportunity is ever lost; someone else will always pick up those you miss.

In describing an opportunity you could in many ways compare it to luck. For instance:

The harder we work the luckier we become
The harder we work the more opportunities we find

Some people appear to be luckier than others
Some people appear to have more opportunities than others

A little bit of luck can lead to great achievements
Small opportunities can be the start of great enterprises.

So, like every other aspect of our business we have to work on it, we have to take action if we want something to happen. In the words of Milton Berle, *"If opportunity doesn't knock; build a door!"* And by the way, if you are waiting for opportunity to knock, you are unlikely to hear it if the television is always on. In the United Kingdom the average person spends twenty-five hours each week watching television. Stagnating. Reduce that by just one third and you will have the equivalent of another fifty-two full working days each year to make and to find new opportunities.

Selling is a proactive business, opportunities abound, but you always have to take the initiative, and you have to be prepared to take a chance, to expose yourself to the risk of succeeding. It is interesting to note that the Chinese word for crisis consists of two characters, the first represents danger and the second represents opportunity. The two are inextricably combined and in every opportunity you will find an element of danger. That is why opportunities are often seen as problems and obstacles. You have to overcome that dangerous element in order to take advantage of the opportunity.

Stepping into dangerous or unfamiliar territory can be intimidating and not everybody will take that step. For many the best place to stay is in the safety of their comfort zone. That is not an area frequented by the opportunist or the entrepreneur. If you want to be successful in your business you must be prepared to take that step and to develop the habit of doing what the unsuccessful people do not like to do.

27

OBJECTIONS

"As in a game of cards, so in the game of life we must play with what is dealt out to us; and the glory consists not so much in winning as in playing a poor hand well". - Josh Billings

Objections are simply requests for reassurance. This means that if you can answer all the objections **to the client's satisfaction,** you will have reassured him and there is every likelihood that you will make the sale. If you are unable to answer the objections satisfactorily it will probably be for one of two reasons. Firstly, because there is a genuine mismatch and your product does not match his requirements. Secondly, you have insufficient knowledge of your product. In either case it is very unlikely that you will make a sale.

In my experience, the best way to deal with an objection is to raise it yourself, before your client does. Initially, that may seem like a strange comment to make but if you think it through you will realise it is the logical solution. You know your product inside out, you know what potential objections a client might have, you have time to prepare your presentation to cover these objections, and you have the opportunity to alleviate your clients concerns before they arise.

As an example we will assume that you have decided price is likely to be an objection. The first thing to do is to check on the competition. How much do they charge, how does the product compare, what additional benefits can you offer, what sort of service do they provide? Use this information in the main body of your presentation: *"Mr Client, you'll appreciate that our product appears to be the most expensive on the market so let me point out the reasons for that ......"* You then go on to explain about your quality, your service and all the other reasons why although appearing to be the most expensive, you believe it is the best value for money.

Be sure to explain the difference between price and cost. Price is merely what you pay to buy, or lease, the product. Cost is what you pay to use the product throughout its life. For instance, compare the price of cars. The one with the lowest price tag is not necessarily the cheapest. Consider what it might cost to run, how often will it be in for repairs, how often will you have to hire a replacement, how long will it last, what sort of resale value will it have? When all that is taken into consideration, compare the average annual cost over the life of the seemingly cheap car with the same costs for the one with the more expensive price tag. Cheap does not always mean inexpensive.

When a client does raise an objection, answer it and confirm that he fully understands and accepts your explanation. If it is something you are going to cover at a later stage in your presentation, ask him if it will be OK to answer it in a few minutes. Whatever you do, do not forget to answer it, and do not ignore it or the client will feel you have something to hide and you will lose his trust.

The professional salesman welcomes objections, it shows the client is concentrating on what you have to say. If there are no objections forthcoming, there is every possibility that the client has his mind elsewhere, and if that is the case there is very little chance of making the sale. If you think this may be the case, find out by asking a question along the lines of: *"Mr Client, how do you feel that would work in your situation?"* or *"Mr Client, can you see any problems with that?"* The answers to those questions will tell you whether he has understood what you are saying, and what his thoughts are concerning the product.

Do not confuse objections with excuses, they are very different. Excuses are used when the client wants to find a way out of buying but is hesitant to say "No". Like most salesmen, I would much prefer to hear somebody say "No" than to be taken for a ride with a plethora of senseless excuses. For this reason I usually tell my clients *"If you feel this is not for you, please let me know. And don't worry, we've been specially trained not to break down and cry if somebody says No!"* That usually raises a chuckle so it helps to relax the client as well as giving him a way out at any point if he wants to take it. A comment like that also puts you in a very strong position as it shows you are not desperate for the business, and that you have his interests at heart.

You can spot the difference between objections and excuses quite easily. Objections in the main are based on reason, whilst excuses are usually very nebulous. Objections for instance are likely to centre around such areas as the quality of your product, the price, service, delivery, size, reliability, colour, etc. An excuse on the other hand will have very little of substance to back it up and will usually disappear when you ask for clarification: *"That's an interesting comment Mr Client, why do you say that?", or "That's an interesting question Mr Client, are there any other areas that you're concerned about?".*

One topic missing from this book is "closing". That is because I believe there will never be a need to "close" if you are selling the right product to the right person, and you accept his objections for what they are, requests for reassurance. The completion of the sale will be an obvious and logical conclusion of your presentation.

28

PERSISTENCE

"Nothing in the world can take the place of persistence. Talent will not; nothing is more common than unsuccessful men with talent. Genius will not; unrewarded genius is almost a proverb. Education will not; the world is full of educated derelicts. Persistence and determination alone are omnipotent". - Calvin Coolidge

At the height of America's great depression in the 1930's successful small businesses were few and far between. One that bucked the trend, however, was a restaurant on the outskirts of Corbin, a small town in the state of Kentucky. Fried chicken was a common enough meal in those days, but the way Colonel Harland Sanders prepared the chicken for his restaurant made it particularly popular.

It was a valuable business and one which the Colonel had every intention of selling when he reached retirement age. He expected to get a good price which would allow him to live his life out in comfort. He had reckoned, however, without the road building programme which was under way at the time. When Interstate 75 opened up, skirting Corbin on its route north to Lexington it took away Colonel Sanders' passing trade and put him out of business.

Sixty-five years old and with no income he knew he had to do something. He checked his assets, virtually all he had now was an old car, a worthless piece of real estate and a recipe for fried chicken. He approached other restaurateurs and offered them his recipe in exchange for a share of the additional profits he told them they would make if they used it. Perhaps it was not surprising that he was turned down. Most restaurants in that area had their own recipe and already sold fried chicken.

Why would they want to pay somebody for something they felt they already had?

Rejection can be very tough to accept and after being turned down a few times most people would probably have gone along with that thinking and given up. After all they were in the middle of the greatest depression the country had ever known. Colonel Sanders was not like most people however, he decided to keep going. He believed in his product and he believed that whoever agreed to his proposal would make money, which meant that the Colonel would also make money.

He travelled throughout the state, on some occasions sleeping in the back of his car, and approaching restaurants everywhere he went. The response was always the same until, eventually, after hearing more than 1000 people say *"NO"*, he eventually got a *"YES"*. He was back in business and his recipe did exactly what he said it would do. It made money for the franchisee, it made money for the Colonel and it provided a tasty meal for the customers, everyone was a winner. He took this information and, with his enthusiasm greater than ever, he went on to sell the same idea to hundreds of others. His persistence had paid off.

That was the start of the company we now know

as Kentucky Fried Chicken and the rest of the story is history. KFC now serves the Colonel's recipe to millions of people all over the world. As Calvin Coolidge said, nothing can take the place of persistence.

The moral of the story, of course, is never give up. In business, sometimes, prospects may seem darkest when really they are on the turn. A little more persistence, a little more effort, and what seemed hopeless failure may turn to glorious success.

Every call you make, on the telephone or in person, is new. OK, you may have had negative responses from everybody you have spoken to today, perhaps even everybody you have spoken to all week, but the client at your next call does not know this. Every call is a new opportunity, but only if you maintain your enthusiasm and your persistence.

Selling is a great profession to be in, it is interesting and it is rewarding. But it can also be tough, sometimes it can be lonely, and occasionally it can be demoralising, if you allow it to be. Remember, nothing worthwhile is ever achieved without effort, and that which we obtain too easily, we regard too lightly. It is difficulty and the hardship which gives everything its value. Besides, if selling was easy there would not have been any jobs when you applied.

Not everybody wants your product, and of those who do want it, not everybody wants it today. This means that you will always get more negative responses than positive ones. But they are not saying *"No"* to you; they are saying *"No"* to the product, *"No, I don't need it at this time"*. They may want it next time so call back on a regular basis until they say they do not want you to call again. Persistence means being tenacious, it does not mean being stubborn or making a nuisance of yourself.

29

PRESENTATION SKILLS

"He who speaks without modesty will find it difficult to make his words good". - Confucius

Selling is very often executed on a one-to-one basis. Often, but not always. There will be times when you find it is necessary to present your product or service to a group. This could be six people, or sixty or six hundred, but the same rules apply whatever the number. And for some people the same fears will also apply. In fact, according to various surveys, there are many people who fear Public Speaking, another name for group presentations, even more than dying. Not exactly rational perhaps, but nonetheless true, and I believe the reason for the fear is the same in both cases, it is simply a fear of the unknown.

And therein lies the difference between the experienced speaker and the novice, the difference that enables one of them to face an audience with confidence, while the other takes on the appearance of a shivering mass of jelly. If you are to move out of the jelly stage and replace it with confidence the first step is to copy the experienced speaker.

You see, an experienced speaker would never allow himself to enter the unknown. His experience would warn him of the potential dangers, and there could be many. His experience would also remind him of the most important aspects of public speaking. What, as an aide memoir, I like to call the 6 P's, the 3 Know's and the 2 R's.

The 6 P's of course are that Proper Prior Preparation Prevents Poor Performance. And the 3 Know's? Number one: Know your audience. Number two: Know your subject. And number three: Know your talk. And, although it may be mathematically incorrect, between them they all add up to the same thing: the two R's. Research and Rehearse.

Know your audience so the talk can be delivered at the right level. Talk down to an audience or pitch it at a level which insults their intelligence and you simply alienate them. So research is vital. What age group do they fall into, are they predominantly male or female, are they there voluntarily, or under duress? In other words do they want to listen to what you have to say, or has somebody told them they have to listen to you? Those in the former group will be far more receptive, and those in the latter group will need to be treated with care if you are to get your message home to them.

What time of day will you be speaking, how many people will be there, how big is the venue, will they be able to see your visual aids or your products? It is essential to obtain the answers to all of these questions to help you in determining both the style and the content of your talk.

Know your subject, because if you do not, you will be found out. Again research is vital. Figures must be correct, details must be accurate, and facts of course should be just that. Facts, not guesses, estimates or assumptions. The only thing more embarrassing than listening to a speaker who is clearly out of his depth, is being that speaker. By the way, this should be the easiest part of your presentation. After all, if you do not know your subject, or your product, why are you selling it?

Know your talk, so it can be delivered with clarity, enthusiasm, and confidence. Write it, read it, rehearse it, and if possible, record it. When you have done this, play it back so you can hear how it will sound to others. And remember that the written word is different to the spoken word. The difference will be obvious to you the first time you read your talk out loud. Abbreviations are good examples. For instance, although we write *"do not"*, we do not say *"do not"*; we say *"don't"*. And although we write *"will not"*, we will not say *"will not"*; we'll say *"won't"*.

Having rehearsed it, and rehearsed it, and rehearsed it, remember it. And when it comes to delivering it, do not read it. Make notes which you can refer to, but do not bury your head in a full manuscript. If you do, it will be impossible to make, or maintain, eye contact with your audience, and again you will alienate them. Nobody likes to be lectured and simple notes or bullet points will ensure you look at your audience and you speak to them in your normal everyday style

Do not apologise. When a speaker says *"I'm not really an expert on this"* or *"I'm sorry if this is going to be boring"* or *"Please excuse me, but I'm very nervous"*, or anything else of that nature, the audience just switches off. Well, would you want to listen to somebody who has just told you that he does not know what he is talking about, or that he is going to be boring?

Approach the lectern, if there is one, with certainty, take your time, gather your thoughts, look at your audience and then open your talk with impact. Use an opening phrase that will capture the attention of your audience from the word go. If you are at the top end of the market you may decide to start with something like *"Ladies and Gentlemen, what I'm going to show you today is the most expensive widget you've ever seen"*. If your audience was expecting you to be defensive about price you will certainly have got their attention as you go on to explain about the quality, the guarantees and the service that also makes it the best value.

Face your audience with confidence; if you want to go out in front, close to your audience, then go out there and talk to them. On the other hand, if you feel happier at a lectern or a podium, then step back behind it. You are giving the talk, you are in control, you make the decision.

Dress suitably. Although jeans would clearly be out of place at the Lord Mayors Banquet, it does not necessarily mean you should dress like your audience. If you were addressing a group of engineering workers in their boiler suits, they would not expect you to be dressed the same. People have an expectation of how others should dress and it can make them feel ill at ease if you do not conform to their expectations.

Would you have confidence in a surgeon if he appeared in the theatre wearing a hard hat and safety boots? Or would you trust a bricklayer to build your house if he came to work in green overalls and rubber gloves. For a business presentation you should always dress in a business like style.

If you are using visual aids, be very careful with the volume of text you use. Slides are there to illustrate and to punctuate your talk. They are not there to read to the audience. Use bullet points which emphasise important aspects of your presentation and at the same time provide you with prompts for your talk!. The golden rule is no more than six lines on any slide, and no more than six words on any line. Any more than this and the slides get confusing.

Most important of all, be natural, be sincere, and be yourself. And one final point; look for a way to finish your talk by saying something other than *Thank you!*

30

QUESTIONS

"I keep six honest serving men,
They taught me all I knew,
Their names are What and Where and When
And How and Why and Who".
- Rudyard Kipling

Questions are the lifeblood of any conversation and any sales interview. Without questions we have no way of knowing what our client wants, what his problems are or if he understands what we are saying. The quality of the answers we get, however, will depend on the quality of the questions we ask, and how we ask them.

Contrary to popular opinion, the science of selling is not talking, it is listening. In order to have something to listen too however, you must be constantly asking questions. To open up a dialogue with your client there is one golden rule: never ask a question to which the answer could be either *"Yes"* or *"No"*. If you do, you will simply shut the conversation down.

Perhaps the worst offenders in this area are the shop assistants. I hesitate to call them retail sales staff as, in the main, they fit better into the category of order taker. The most common form of greeting by these assistants is *"Can I help you?"* and the most common reply is *"No, thank you!".* End of conversation. With that response there is no opportunity to talk to the client or to sell him one of your products.

How much better to greet your prospective customer with something like *"Where are you thinking of using this product?"* or *"Which of these looks like it would suit your requirements?"* or *"What model do you use at the moment?".* Any one of those questions could start a conversation which would allow you to determine whether or not the product is right for the individual. If it is, then the conversation could lead you naturally into your sales presentation. If it is not you can say *"Good Day"* and turn your attention to more productive areas.

The two sets of questions we have just used fall into two distinct categories. To find out if you understand what the categories are I could ask you *"Do you know the difference?"* or *"Will you explain the difference to me?"* The first of those is a *"Closed"* question which only requires a one word answer and allows the conversation to be closed down instantly. The second one is an *"Open"* question which has to be answered with a statement. When your client answers with a statement it provides you with an opportunity to progress quite naturally to a conversation.

Closed questions have no place in the vocabulary of a professional salesman. Leave them to the order takers. On the other hand, it may well be that you will find yourself at the receiving end of a closed question from time to time. After all, not everybody has your skills! When that does happen, be ready and do not fall into the trap of answering in a closed manner. Turn the question around. By answering a question with a question you can open a dialogue and give yourself an opportunity to present the benefits of your product or service.

Here are a few very simple examples of turning a question around:

Q. *"Do you have this in red?"*
A. *"How many do you want in red?"*
Q. *"How long is delivery on this?"*
A. *"When do you want it for?"*
Q. *"Will your widget do this task?"*
A. *"That's an interesting question, why do you ask?"*

Simple and to the point, none of those replies could sensibly be answered with a *"Yes"* or a *"No"*. Such questions, and dozens of others like them, will provide you with the opening to start the conversation flowing in the direction you want to go.

Incidentally, when you acquire this skill, do not limit it to selling or to business. You can make equally good use of it in social circumstances and personal relationships. Even that tired old classic *"Do you come here often?"* can be replaced with something along the lines of *"What made you decide to come here today?"*. And with just a little bit of thought and planning you will find many more and many better ways to open up your conversations in every situation.

We said at the beginning of this chapter that the science of selling is listening. If you really want to do some listening, present your client with an opportunity to talk about himself. People like nothing better than talking about their success and their life.

"Tell me Mr Client, how did you get started in this business?".

"When you started the business how did you attract your first customers?".

"How do you deal with your competition?".

"How did you get into the export market?".

They are all open questions designed to get the conversation off to a flying start, and, again, none of them can be answered with a *"Yes"* or a *"No"*.

31

RECORDS

"Besides the noble art of getting things done, there is the noble art of leaving things undone. The wisdom of life consists in the elimination of non essentials". - Lin Yutang

The aim in business, as in all the other areas of your life, should be to constantly improve. In order to do this you have to measure your performance and evaluate it against your previous achievements. This means keeping records of your statistics.

How many telephone calls do you make, how many appointments do you make, how many appointments are kept, how many presentations do you make, how many sales do you make, how many introductions do you obtain? What is your ratio of 'phone calls to appointments, appointments to presentations, presentations to sales? What is the average size of your sale, which product do you sell most of, which do you sell least of? Are you more successful in the morning or the afternoon, early in the week or towards the end of the week? Do you get more introductions from new clients or existing clients?

All of these figures, and many more, will provide you with valuable information which will allow you to measure your performance and your improvement.

If you are most successful in making sales during the first part of the week then make sure that the majority of your selling appointments are arranged for the early part of the week. Keep the later part of the week for catching up on paper work, preparing your presentations, reviews, etc. The only way you will know this is by keeping records.

Prepare a simple matrix to keep track of your activity and fill it in every day. Look at the example I have included in this chapter and use that as a starting point. See how you could adapt it to suit your business. Do you need to include any other headings, or change some of those I have included? This is a record of your activity and your performance. It is for your benefit, you are the only one who will be using it, so you decide what should be included.

Do not just aim for a big improvement in one area and ignore the others. It is far more effective, and far more productive, to aim for small improvements in every area. For instance, if you improve you ratio of appointments to 'phone calls by 50%, it simply means you will see 50% more people. It does not mean you will be more effective when you see those people. If, on the other hand, you show a modest 3% improvement in five different areas such as telephone approaches, appointments kept, presentations made, sales completed and average sale size , your overall effectiveness will improve by a massive 243% (3x3x3x3x3).

Do not stop there. Aim for constant refinement and constant improvement, working on every area, all the time. There is always room for further improvement. Use your records when business slows down and you find yourself heading for a trough. Your figures will give you early warning and help you minimise the problem. What were your figures like the last time business took a downturn? What did you change to climb back up? Provided your records are accurate, all the answers will be there.

Review your records on a regular basis; at least every month and possibly every week. Look out for areas which need your attention and make sure they get that attention. Compare your statistics with those of a colleague, or with team averages. How do you stack-up in each area, and overall? What are your strong points and what are your weak points? Do not make the classic mistake of working on your weaknesses and ignoring your strengths. Wherever possible you should delegate your weaknesses and major on your strengths.

ACTIVITY ANALYSIS

Week ending:	1 'PHONE CALLS	2 APPOINTMENTS MADE	3 APPOINTMENTS KEPT	4 PRESENTATIONS	5 NUMBER OF SALES	6 VALUE OF SALES	7 AVERAGE VALUE OF AN APPOINTMENT (6÷3)	8 AVERAGE VALUE OF A SALE (6÷5)	9 INTRODUCTIONS OBTAINED
Monday									
Tuesday									
Wednesday									
Thursday									
Friday									
TOTALS									

Use this to measure your performance and your improvement; transfer the weekly figures to an annual chart to follow your progress.

32

SKILLS

"If a man is called to be a street sweeper, he should sweep streets even as Michelangelo painted, or Beethoven composed music or Shakespeare wrote poetry.
He should sweep streets so well that all the hosts of heaven and earth will pause to say here lived a great street sweeper who did his job well". - Martin Luther King Jr

Skills is (alphabetically) the final part of a mnemonic which we looked at in earlier chapters. KASH refers to the Knowledge, Attitude, Skills and Habits which are essential to our success, in sales or any other area of our life. Knowledge, Attitude and Habits have already been covered which means it is time to complete the series.

By skills we normally mean selling skills and those needed are many and varied. Marketing skills, listening skills, communication skills, learning skills, presentation skills, and many more, all equally important. Sharpening all of those skills should be high on your list of priorities. The best marketing plan in the world will fail to produce any business if the salesman has no other skills and no matter how many clients he sees, he will struggle to communicate if he is unable to build rapport.

One very effective way to sharpen those skills is

to work with a colleague for a few weeks as we suggested in the chapter on habits. Analyse each others strengths and weaknesses. Decide which of your skills need to be honed, and do something about them. Attend seminars, enrol in classes, read books, listen to tapes, it does not matter which route you take so long as you take some positive action. To keep your skills razor sharp you have to work on them constantly throughout your career.

Prepare a matrix similar to the one we used in the section on record keeping. Use this one to show which areas are in need of some attention and which areas are improving. You may want to complete this each week, each month, or even each quarter. I would recommend that you do not have longer intervals than quarterly or you will allow too much time for things to drift off track. In the example on page 109 I have assumed a two monthly check and have only used a few skill areas, you will obviously wish to include many more and tailor it to suit your own individual situation.

Mark each category out of ten and chart your progress throughout the year. This will tell you which areas you need to work on and which areas you are making progress in. For a comparison, use two of these and pass the second one on to your colleague to complete. You may be surprised by how other people's perception of your abilities differs greatly to your own. Do not dismiss their views as incorrect, that is how the world sees you.

A great deal of time and energy can be wasted by attempting to *re-invent the wheel;* by looking for the answer to something that has already been discovered elsewhere. Make use of existing knowledge and the existing skills of others by using the NLP technique of *Modelling.* This simply involves finding somebody

SKILL AREA	JAN	MAR	MAY	JULY	SEPT	NOV
Telephone Skills						
Presentation Skills						
Listening Skills						
Communication Skills						
Rapport Building						
Service Charter						
Record Keeping						
Time Management						

who has the skill you want to develop, and copying him. Speak to him, ask him about his attitude to that particular skill, ask him what he does to keep it sharp, watch how he uses his skill, find out as much as you can and then duplicate it.

If you want to sharpen up your telephone skills, listen to an expert making his calls. Write down what he says, especially any standard phraseology he uses. Listen to the pitch and the pace of his voice. What sort of overall impression does he convey? Is he clinically efficient or relaxed and friendly? Listen to how he handles queries or objections and then ask him afterwards what had been said by the person at the other end. Ask him what his attitude is to objections on the telephone. In other words, find out everything you possibly can about his telephone technique and then reproduce it.

Do not spend all your time on perfecting one skill. As we said in the chapter on Records, improving each area by a little will be far more effective than improving one area by a lot.

33

TIME MANAGEMENT

"Punctuality is the politeness of Kings". - Louis XVIII

Although I cannot vouch through personal experience for the accuracy of the comment above by King Louis, I can guarantee that punctuality is the politeness of salesmen. When a client agrees to invest his valuable time by seeing you, you are duty bound to him not to waste that time by keeping him waiting. Punctuality is an area where you can show your professionalism to everybody you meet, every day of the week. But of course good timekeeping when we are meeting clients is only part of time management.

There is one thing about time management, or time control, that you must understand at the outset. Each day has twenty-four hours, each hour has sixty minutes and each minute has sixty seconds. No amount of planning or training will ever change that! If the job you are working on will take an hour to complete and you have allocated sixty minutes for it, you will be able to complete it. If the job will take two hours and you have allocated sixty minutes for it, you will not be able to complete it.

Perhaps I am in danger of stating the obvious here, but I have met many people on my courses who believe that somehow good time management will allow them to stretch the available time. Take my word for it, that will not happen! What good time management will do is ensure you complete the most important things in the time that is available. Do you remember what we said in the chapter on Activity? *"Only do what only you can do".* Everything else should be delegated.

There are various systems for making sure the important things get done first. The best one I have seen is very simple. It consists of three things, a list divided into three columns, the ten day follow up system which we looked at in an earlier chapter, and the Yellow Box Diary system which we will look at in a later chapter. As I said before, everything is based on the premise that if you are going to do a job properly, you can only concentrate on one job at a time.

There is nothing hi-tech about the list, all you need is an A4 pad, a ruler and a pen. Divide the paper into three equal columns - A, B, and C. Then write down all the jobs you have to do, categorising them as you write them. Column "A" is only for jobs that have to be done today. "B" and "C" are for everything else, in order of importance. Incidentally, you must decide which jobs are most important for you, and where they go on the list.

Having prepared your list, start work on the first item and ignore everything else until you have completed it. Do not allow yourself to be interrupted by telephone calls. Ask someone to take messages and let your caller know that you will get back to them. As you will see when we look at the diary, there will be a time for telephone calls, a time that suits you. When you have completed the first task on your "A" list, proceed to the next one. When the "A" list has been completed, move on to column "B", select the most important task and go to work on it.

If you cannot clear your list by that method it is very unlikely that you could clear it by any other method. But you will have spent your time constructively, working on the most important items and any other method probably would have taken longer. When you follow this system, you are making the most of the time available to you and that is good time management. Before you finish work each day, review your list, re-write it and re-categorise any items which have not been completed so you are ready to start again on the next day.

If you never have sufficient time to get through your "A" list, your problem is not time management. In this situation you need to look more carefully at your list to see what else can be delegated. You are unique and you have special qualities but do not fall into the trap of believing that nobody else is capable of doing a good job. For instance, if there is a lot of work to do in preparing a presentation for an important client you may feel it is too important to be left to anybody else. You are right, such a document does need your special input, but you do not have to do the research and you do not have to prepare the draft.

Give a project of this nature to someone else and let them spend the necessary hours getting it ready. You will find that when people are given responsibility they invariably rise to the occasion. It is only necessary for you to step in at the final stage and make, or dictate, any changes which you feel are needed. It is far easier to edit than it is to originate. It is also a lot less time consuming and therefore allows you to be more creative as you are not bogged down by the mundane tasks.

Time really is money and as we cannot stretch it,

we must use it productively. Imagine the time available to you was like your bank account and you had to write a cheque whenever you used some of it. Would you be happy to write a cheque for idle gossip around the coffee machine? Would you gladly write a cheque for a wasted journey because you had not confirmed your appointment before leaving?

Counting time will never be as important as making time count, using it constructively and efficiently. When you are busy and productive time flies by but if you do ever find that time is dragging, remember that the best way to kill time is to work it to death.

34

U.S.P.

"Fear less, hope more; eat less, chew more; whine less, breathe more; hate less, love more; and all good things are yours". - Swedish Proverb

USP is the acronym used in sales for your Unique Selling Point or Proposition. Your product or service is different to that of your competitors, and that difference is your unique selling point. It is what distinguishes you, your company and your product from all the others.

As we are talking about something unique it will clearly be different for everybody. This means that if you are to use this unique distinction to your advantage the first thing you must do is to identify it. For this you need to look carefully at every feature, compare your product with others on the market. What is it that is different, what is it that is better, what is it specifically that your clients like about it?

Is it the quality, the materials, the delivery, the style, the price, the guarantee, the colour, the durability, the purity, the advertising, the popularity, the exclusivity, the demand, the flexibility, the name? Or is it the back-up, the payment terms, the service, the running costs? Or is it a combination of more than one of these?

Until you know what it is you will not be able to take advantage of it. There is one USP however that you can identify very quickly and very clearly by simply looking in the mirror. You! You will always be your most unique selling point. Although there are millions of people in our world, your creator thought so much of you, he only made one. You are the same you that you have always been so you may not feel that there is anything special about you. There is! Do not waste it! Capitalise on that unique identity and develop it!

You have a style and personality like no one else. Your level of knowledge and skill, your ability and attitude, your character and competence are shared by no one. How do others perceive those points? Of course they see them as different but do they also see them in a positive light. In the chapters on Records and Skills we talked about identifying your abilities in certain aspects of business. Now you need to take a closer, more personal, look at yourself to see what development or change might be needed on a personal level.

Consider every viewpoint. What is the first impression people have when they meet you. Are you quiet and reticent so people cannot see your confidence and therefore cannot put their confidence in you? Are you bombastic and flamboyant to the point where people become nervous in your company and therefore would find it difficult to build a relationship? Do you monopolise the conversation or do you hold back so people have to elicit information from you?

Ask the questions and be true to yourself. Sometimes the answers may not be what you **want** to hear but in those cases they are most likely to be what you **need** to hear. When you know what needs changing treat it like any other aspect of your business. Set targets and decide on a time scale for the change to take place. Again, you can use the broad concept in doing this: "Where am I now?" "Where do I want to be?" "What methods are there of getting there?" "Which is the best for me right now?"

"You never get a second chance to make a good first impression". That saying has been around for years, I have used it elsewhere in this book and I am sure that you have heard it on numerous occasions. That means it has stood the test of time, and for the very best of reasons, because it is true. Take a look in the mirror. Is that the impression you want to portray?

Your appearance says a lot about who you are and what your attitude is. Do you look like a professional or does your appearance let you down? It is important that you dress appropriately for the business you are in. Business is not the place to parade your latest fashion accessories, that can wait for your leisure time. People expect certain standards and if you do not conform to them you run the risk of creating a poor impression.

Of course there are always exceptions to prove the rule and we have all seen successful salesmen who flout the rules to display their individuality. If you want to follow that route the only thing to remember is that the odds are against you. My recommendation is that you do everything possible to stack the odds in your favour. Selling can be a tough business, why create additional problems unnecessarily?

In the majority of situations the accepted dress for a saleswoman is a business suit or a sober dress. The low cut, tight fitting items that are designed to turn heads should be used to turn them outside of business hours. The clothes you wear will provide your client with an instant first impression, and from that he will make long lasting decisions on your ability and your professionalism.

Men should always wear a suit with a shirt and tie. White shirts are the most universally condoned, but blue or striped shirts are generally acceptable. Choose a quality silk tie that holds its shape and with a pattern that will blend in with your suit rather than glare out from behind your jacket. Shoes should always be well polished. Dressing to conform in this manner does not mean you lose you personality, there is still room for that to shine through.

Do not forget the tools of your trade. What sort of brief case do you use? The plastic ones you can buy for give away prices at the local supermarket may carry your papers, but they are hardly likely to impress you client. Use a quality brief case and make sure it is well organised. Do not just throw things into it, your brief case is your mobile office and when you are with a client you should be able to find the item you want without having to scramble about.

Is your car clean and reliable, would you be happy to give your client a lift in it without any prior warning? Do you wear a cheap watch that you got free with a can of oil or one that gives the appearance of price and quality? Do you use a plastic pen with the end chewed away or do you have a quality writing instrument that reflects your professionalism? Little things mean a lot.

When you feel good and look good your confidence increases. When your confidence increases your sales performance improves. When your sales performance is high your confidence increases and you find yourself in an upward spiral of success. Be yourself, stay unique and make the decision to be the best you that you can be.

35

VOCABULARY

"Kind words can be short and easy to speak, but their echoes are endless". - Mother Theresa

Part of the lyric of a very popular song of yesteryear suggested that you should 'accentuate the positive and eliminate the negative.' I use the lyric here as an illustration for the message it conveys because I want to look at words, and in particular the negative words and phrases used in our everyday vocabulary.

I do not profess to know why, but we do have a tendency in this country to use negative expressions as a matter of habit, and it is a habit which I believe we should endeavour to change. The reason for this is that **what** we say and **how** we say it influences both how we feel and how we act. Fortunately we do have a choice, it is up to us whether we choose phraseology which has a negative influence on our behaviour, or phraseology which has a positive influence.

Clearly we should be using the positive type but for some reason I have yet to understand, the other version seems to be more popular. Greet somebody with the usual *"How are you?"*, and the most common reply will be *"Not bad"*. That is a very strange reply, logic determines that if we are not bad, we must be good. That being the case our reply should be positive: *"Very good, thanks"*, *"I'm great"*, *"... wonderful"*, *"... terrific"*, *"... marvellous"*. It is amazing what a difference a response like this makes, to us and to those around us. It creates confidence which will rub off on others and create a more positive environment.

When our clients ask how business is, it is remarkable how many people appear to be almost afraid to tell anybody how well they are doing. Instead they give the same old trite replies:

"... very slow", *"... we're keeping going"* or perhaps, as an attempt at being positive: *"... we're doing as well as can be expected these days"*. It is as though they are looking for sympathy when, instead, they should be looking for business! When business is going well, tell your clients, and everyone else you meet, that *"... business is great"*, or *"... we're having a superb year"*, or whatever else is appropriate. People like to do business with successful people, not with the doom and gloom merchants.

I am not suggesting for one moment that you mislead anybody, if business is not doing very well, do not say it is. That does not mean you have to be negative though. How about saying *".... I'm really busy"*, or *"..... I'm rushed off my feet"*, or *"..... we've never been busier"*. When you tell somebody you are busy, they will automatically assume that you are also successful and, as we said, people like to do business with successful people.

Incidentally, if business is not doing very well and you are not busy, you have just found out why it is not doing well!

One of the problems we face in our attempts to be positive is the media. That is an area that thrives on the negative and shies away from the positive as though it is a plague carrier. This was evidenced some time ago when the television newscaster Martin Lewis was hauled over the coals by his superiors for daring to suggest that news bulletins should include more good news, more positive items. Of course this was a total anathema to the *Powers That Be,* those demi-gods who had spent years steeped in the lore of negativity, so they closed ranks on him.

Yes, the bulk of hard news is negative: war, terrorism, crime and so on, but that doesn't mean it's all doom and gloom.

There is still some good news around but you would have a hard time finding it. Look at virtually any paper, broadsheet or tabloid, and you will see that no matter what the event, the majority of the banner headlines have a negative slant and the worse the news is, the bigger the headline is. The good news, the positive items, will be tucked carefully away at the bottom of the page.

Radio Announcers are no better, I once heard an announcer start his programme by saying: *"Good Monday morning, if there is such a thing!"* Well, of course there is, for me every morning is a good morning. Mondays are marvellous, Tuesdays are terrific, Wednesdays are wonderful, Thursdays are tremendous, Fridays are fabulous, Saturdays are sensational and Sundays are superb. From what I can gather, we are not supposed to enjoy Monday because for most people it means going back to work and it seems that should not be a pleasure. If that is the case, you are in the wrong job.

Even the weather reporters are getting in on the act. During the snow and ice of winter one weatherman reported that it was the worst winter for goodness knows how many years. That was not a fact, that was opinion. A few days earlier I had been talking to a friend who was involved in mountaineering and rock climbing. He told me it was the best winter for goodness knows how many years because there was some great snow for skiing and plenty of ice for ice climbing. The fact is that it was the coldest winter for years, that did not mean it was the worst.

Do not allow yourself to be influenced by this tirade of pessimism. It is of course impossible to avoid the media but it is important that you understand it for what it is. Look and listen for the positive aspects of the news and carry that positive attitude over to your business. As I said, it is our choice, so be sure to make the right one. Forget all the ifs and buts and maybes and make a decision to really eliminate the negative and accentuate the positive.

36

WORRY

"Courage is resistance to fear, mastery of fear; not absence of fear". - Mark Twain

Hand in hand with the joy of selling goes the anxiety and apprehension that have unfortunately become part and parcel of virtually every salesman's life. And yet, this worry, or fear, is totally unjustified. To paraphrase Franklin D Roosevelt's famous statement: *"we have nothing to worry about, except worry itself."*

Making appointments, the salesman worries about every telephone call in anticipation of a negative response even though we all know that by the law of averages, some people will say *"Yes"* and others will say *"No"*. Incidentally, they are not saying *"No"* to us, only to our product at that time. Worry rears its head again at the appointment stage when the concern changes to whether the prospective client will be there and whether he will allow sufficient time for the presentation to be made. And the biggest worry of all salesmen is that the client will change his mind after he has bought the product.

As we said above however, all this worry is uncalled for. Yes, of course all those things, and more, will happen to you from time to time during your sales career, but worrying about them will not change anything. I have known situations where even though I had confirmed an appointment on the 'phone before leaving my office, I arrived thirty minutes later to find the client was not there, he had been called away on an emergency. Worrying about it would not have brought him back.

There have also been instances where the client changed his mind, usually because there had been an unexpected change in his circumstances. Such experiences are frustrating but again, worrying about them in advance will not change the situation. It will change you though. If you spend your time constantly worrying about what might happen next, you will develop a negative attitude which will be picked up by your clients. That will do very little to instill them with confidence in your ability to provide a solution to their problems and as a result your worry will have a negative impact on your business.

Reliable estimates suggest that 40% of the things most people worry about are never likely to happen. For another 30% of those worries it is too late, whatever it is they are worrying about has already happened, there is nothing that can be done about them. A further 12% concerns unfounded health worries which gives some credence to the view that there is a little bit of a hypochondriac in everybody. Trivial, insignificant worries account for another 10%. That brings the total to 92% which means that only 8% of worries have any real foundation.

There is a mnemonic which sums it up very nicely:

False
Expectations
Appearing
Real

You start off by *thinking* a client might say *"No"*, and then build it up in your mind until you reach a point where you are convinced they really will say *"No"*. If you are not careful, this can very easily turn into a self-fulfilling prophecy which means as a result of your own attitude, you will convert those false expectations into reality.

Remember that the function of fear is to warn us of danger, not to make us afraid to face it. Of course there is a possibility that the client will say *"No"* at some point in the sales process. We know that. That possibility is our warning, but there is no need to worry about it if we sincerely believe that our product is right for the client.

It is normally dangerous to make assumptions, but this is the exception which proves the rule! When you are on the telephone, assume the client will say *"Yes"* and assume he will want to meet you to hear what you have to offer. When you arrive for your appointment assume your client will be there, 99% of the time he will be. And assume that he will extend you the courtesy of listening to your presentation, after all, it is unlikely that he would have agreed to the meeting if he did not want to hear what you have to say. These assumptions will help you to develop a positive attitude which will also be picked up by your client and, unlike the negative attitude, is likely to give him confidence in your ability.

As for changing his mind after the sale is made, there is nothing you can do about it at that point. If it happens for a genuine reason, you simply accept it and see if there is any other way in which you can help the client. As a professional salesman, you are not in the business of making one off sales, you want to work with that client for a long time to come.

If he has changed his mind because he finds it is the wrong product, or he has bought too much, or he has been overcharged, or the terms are not what he had understood them to be, or any other similar reason, you have not done your job properly. When you explain everything to his satisfaction and he decides to buy your product, there will never be any need for anxiety or worry about cancellation. Think of worry like a rocking chair, it gives you something to do, but it does not get you anywhere.

37

eXcellence

"The quality of a person's life is in direct proportion to their commitment to excellence, regardless of their chosen endeavour". - Vincent T Lombardi

Excellence should not be seen as something exceptional. Excellence should be your standard, something you aim for in everything you do. In business the professional will never settle for anything less than the best and even though you may not always achieve those heights, the pursuit of excellence will guarantee that you stay out of the depths of mediocrity.

But excellence must mean something, it must be more than just a word in your vocabulary. Aristotle is quoted as saying: *"Excellence is not an art, excellence is a habit".* Make a decision that *"if it's good enough for Aristotle, it's good enough for me"* and make excellence one of our own habits. Your clients deserve the best and you tell them that you will provide them with the best, you can only deliver that promise when you maintain excellence as your standard.

The quality control department is one of the most important in any company, without it customers could receive goods which are below standard and which would do untold harm for the reputation of the company. Such a department should not be exclusive to the company however, quality control is equally important in the businesses of selling when you are aiming for excellence.

Perhaps you are selling a product which has already been through the quality control department and therefore you feel it does not apply to you. Let me assure you, you will never be more wrong about anything in your life. Quality control, delivering a top quality product or service, is the responsibility of everyone connected with every business. A friend of mine, Jim Lawson, simply says *"The alternative to quality is not an option".* Jim is right, we should provide premier quality service as a matter of routine.

Routine is probably a good word to use in this context. The quality control department we mentioned has a system, or a routine, for checking the products, and by going through that routine meticulously they can ensure nothing leaves without being thoroughly checked. Do the same for your service. Install a system that will ensure you follow through with your promises to the client and that your service to him will be second to none.

When your client attempts to contact you, how is his call handled if you are not in the office? Are you able to get back to him within a specified time? What happens if you are unable to contact him within the agreed time? Do you keep your delivery dates? In short, when a client agrees to do business with you, do you ensure that everything you said would happen, does happen?

If you do not know the answers to all of those questions, you are not providing the client with the service he deserves. You should know the answers to all the questions concerning the level of service provided by your business. When you are not in the office, leave instructions as to how a client's call should be handled. It may simply be that somebody will take a message and advise the client that you will call back. If you are likely to be out of the office for a few days make sure that somebody else contacts the clients on your behalf, or that you 'phone in regularly for your messages.

When you collect your messages get in touch with the client, even if it is only to say you are out of the office and will deal with his query as soon as you are back at your desk. If you do not call him, he may think you have not received the message, or worse still he may think you have ignored the message. His concern will then increase to the point where eventually what started out as a minor query will end up as a major problem in his mind. Have the courtesy to let him know his call is important and you are doing something about it.

It is often said that real service begins where lip service ends. In other words, it is no use talking about it, for service to mean anything you have to do something about it. It is no use you saying you provide an excellent service; it is only happening when your client says your service is excellent. What do we mean by service? It is going beyond the sale, going the extra mile after the sale is made, caring for our clients needs. It is an intangible, and it is a distinguishing feature of a professional salesman.

The quality of your service will determine the quality of your sales. First class clients demand, and deserve, first class service. If you are unable, or unprepared, to provide it, you are in the wrong business. In fact, if you do not provide an excellent level of service you will not be in business! Somebody else will be prepared to make the extra effort and will jump in front of you.

Give your client a service commitment. For instance, I believe all calls should be returned within forty-eight hours but even if you have to make this seventy-two hours, make sure you stick to it. Broken promises can rarely be mended. If you have promised to do something within a specified time and it later proves impossible to fulfil, make sure you let him know. He may not be overjoyed at the thought of a delay, but at least he will appreciate that you have not just ignored him.

Think for a moment. If somebody else was providing you with the level of service you provide for your clients, would you feel short changed. If the answer is *"No"*, you probably have not thought hard enough. There is always room for improvement, there is always something you could do better. I am not suggesting you aim for perfection, but I am recommending you strive for excellence. That is not easy, it will require a good deal of effort and determination on your part. But nobody ever said this business was easy. If it was easy it would not be so rewarding.

38

YELLOW BOX DIARY SYSTEM

"Lost, yesterday, somewhere between sunrise and sunset, two golden hours, each set with sixty diamond minutes. No reward is offered for they are gone forever". - Horace Mann

The Yellow Box Diary System is a very simple and effective method of controlling the use of your time and should be used in conjunction with the Follow Up and Time Management systems from earlier chapters. It enables you to plan your time effectively and has the added bonus of increasing the number of appointments you make.

Before you even open your diary, make a list of all the tasks you have to carry out during your normal working day. These might include telephoning, preparation of presentations or proposals, answering correspondence, planning, study, general administration, sales meetings, staff meetings, presentations to clients and so on. In preparing this list bear in mind that you are looking for tasks that YOU have to do, ignore all those tasks which can be delegated. Having compiled the list go through it with a fine tooth comb and see if any more of those tasks can be delegated. Remember; *"Only do what only you can do".*

Now re-write your list putting everything in order of importance. If presenting to clients, and telephoning to arrange meetings are not right at the top of the list, start again because you have got it wrong! Of course you cannot ignore such vital ingredients as planning and preparation but if you are not seeing the people, there will be nothing to plan and nothing to prepare for. You will only make a sale when you are talking to the client and you will only get a chance to talk to the client when you arrange a meeting.

The next step in the process is to allocate time to each task. How much of your day do you need to spend with clients? In order to meet those clients how much time will you need to spend on the telephone arranging the meetings? How much does that leave, because everything else has got to be fitted in to the time that is left over when you have completed that exercise. If there is not enough time left for all the other tasks you will have to review your list again and do some more delegating.

Now you can open your diary and using a yellow highlighter, block out the times you want to allocate for client meetings. Then use a different colour to block out your telephone time. Nothing else gets done during those hours; your planning, preparation and all the other tasks are allocated times of their own. If you are working on something and the time arrives for, say, telephoning, stop what you are doing and pick up the 'phone.

You will have to be very strict with yourself or the system will not work.

If you are accustomed to letting your clients choose the time, or just slotting meetings into any apparently spare space, you may initially find this system a little strange and perhaps even restrictive.

Persevere, like all good things, it is worth spending the time to get it right. Let your clients know what times you are available for meetings and, whatever you do, do not deviate from the yellow boxes. Speak with confidence and you will find the clients are generally happy to go along with your suggestions.

Make sure there is enough space for your target number of meetings at the times you want those meetings, not the times you normally make them or the times you think your clients will be available. To control your time efficiently, the decision on when to do things has to be made by you That is too important a decision to be left to anybody else.

Not only will this system make you more efficient, but it will actually increase the number of appointments you make. I cannot tell you how this happens, but I can tell you that it does. You may recall a scene in the movie *Field Of Dreams* when the guy was told to build a baseball field beside his house. Speaking of the old time player, Shoeless Joe, a voice told him to *"... build it and he will come".* The field was built and, as promised, Shoeless Joe turned up. Our diaries seem to work in much the same way. When we make space for something it fills up.

This system has worked for numerous people selling all kinds of products and services but what you want to know is, will it work for you? I believe it will, but do not simply accept my word for it, if you have any doubts do it for yourself and judge for yourself. Make it a habit, and review your success after three months. You have nothing to lose. As always of course, it will only work when you take action.

39

ZEAL

"Look at a day when you are supremely satisfied at the end. It's not a day when you lounge around doing nothing; it's when you've had everything to do, and you've done it". - Margaret Thatcher

Zeal is described in the dictionary as *"eager enthusiasm"* and *"eager desire or effort"*. I cannot imagine a better description of how we should go about our business. And what a marvellous note on which to finish this book. We started with Activity and Attitude, add Zeal to those two attributes and we could almost forget the other twenty-four letters that are in between.

It has often been said that the sale is made before the client even knows what you are selling, that your clients buy you before they buy your product or service. For that to happen, however, you must go about your business with that eager enthusiasm and show your eager desire to put the interests of your clients first by providing them with the service they want. This means exhibiting zeal without becoming a zealot, knowing when to ease off, and understanding the difference between providing a service and becoming a nuisance.

More than one salesman has lost clients simply by

being over zealous, by pestering their clients when they thought they were helping them. Selling is our business and will always be more important to us than it will be to our clients. It is not the only thing on which they have to spend their time and if we waste their time we will be giving them a very good reason to look for an alternative provider. Unannounced visits from us or appointments arranged for no good reason will certainly not put us high on their list of favourite people. Act in a professional manner, never force the situation and never outstay your welcome.

It is not an easy blend, and it may even sound like a contradiction, but when we learn to combine the virtue of patience with our eager enthusiasm, we will have a very powerful combination indeed. To do this we must become active listeners, always listening instead of simply waiting for our turn to speak. This way we will not only hear what our clients say, we will also understand what they mean and, as a result, be in a position to provide them with the service they want.

Build a genuine empathy with your clients that will show them you care. Look out for opportunities, not only opportunities to increase your business, but opportunities to help your clients even when it does not produce business. Display the enthusiasm which will see you through the bad times as well as the good.

This eager desire and enthusiasm should also extend to your daily activities. You should be a salesman because you want to be one, because you enjoy it and because you want to provide a service for others. If you join the business because there were no other jobs, or you thought it was well paid, or because it provides a company car you will not enjoy it and without that enjoyment you will struggle to display enthusiastic eagerness.

A question I am often asked by people considering selling as a career is whether it is an easy job. My answer is *"Yes"*. Yes, selling is easy when you work hard, but it is very hard when you attempt to take it easy. Physically it is not particularly demanding, but mentally it can be extremely strenuous. It can also be a very lonely job as you often spend days on end away from your colleagues on the road. You meet plenty of people of course, but you meet them all in a business situation which can be very tense.

Much of this tension can be relieved by your zeal for the job. It is rarely a taxing experience to spend your time engaged in an activity which you enjoy. This does not mean things will go smoothly all the time. There will be occasions for everybody where things go badly even to the point where you may feel like looking for a new career. That happens in every business, in fact it happens in every facet of our lives. In such a situation it is your genuine interest and enthusiasm that will provide the boost to get you back on track.

Direct your zeal towards becoming more professional every day you do the job. Most important of all, enjoy your life in sales, it is a great career with unlimited opportunities. It offers the sort of variety not seen in any other business and it allows you to be directly rewarded for your efforts.

Good luck.